THE DOMINICA

The Dominican Way

EDITED BY LUCETTE VERBOVEN

continuum

Published by the Continuum International Publishing Group

The Tower Building	80 Maiden Lane
11 York Road	Suite 704
London	New York
SE1 7NX	NY 10038

www.continuumbooks.com

First published 2011

British Library Cataloguing-in-Publication Data
A catalogue record for this book is available from the British Library.

ISBN: 978-0-8264-4277-2

Typeset by Fakenham Prepress Solutions, Fakenham, Norfolk, NR21 8NN
Printed and bound in India

For my mother,
who danced and prayed
her way through life

Contents

Acknowledgements

This book owes its existence to the obliging cooperation of the nine men and eight women who accepted to be interviewed by me, kindly showing me their world – be it the cloister, the open field or the confines of a laboratory. At the outset of this project, I already had a sense of the charism of the Dominicans but I had no idea that it could run so deep. I am greatly indebted to the then Master of the Order, Brother Carlos Azpiroz Costa, and the members of the General Council who helped me to identify brothers and sisters to be interviewed.

I am profoundly grateful for the invaluable help and advice of Timothy Radcliffe, whom I first interviewed some 15 years ago in the Santa Sabina for an international television series. It was Timothy who sowed the first seed of this project. Since then, my interviews have multiplied, but somehow I always seemed to return to him and the Dominicans. So, it was inevitable that the time would come to write a book about this Dominican way. Timothy introduced the concept to Robin Baird-Smith, Publishing Director of Continuum, and off we went!

I am most grateful to Robin, who has been the perfect guide for this challenging project. He always found the right tone to encourage me on my way and thus gently supported the birth of this book.

This book would not have been possible without the practical help of two great people: Milou Bodifée and Helen Titchen Beeth. My lovely sister-in-law, Milou, patiently typed out all the interviews, a truly demanding task, which she performed with great care. Helen acted as my language consultant, checking the texts and providing English versions of interviews that had originally been in French or Dutch.

My special thanks also to Toon Osaer, Managing Director of Catholic Television Belgium who made it possible to broadcast the interviews with Radcliffe, Alford, Nzamujo and Burin des Roziers. I also owe thanks to the Artistic Director of this television series, Dominik Vanheusden.

I am especially grateful to two people. My mother, who passed away just a few days before the start of the project, has always been a loving presence and a stimulating force for me. She sensed what authentic religion should be and did not necessarily conform to what was expected of her. She applauded this project, but couldn't see the end of it.

My beloved husband, Gerard Bodifée, the most important person in my life, has been a keen supporter from the start. Being an author himself, he has been a wonderful coach and we talked about the interviewees as if they were guests at our dinner table.

Introduction

TIMOTHY RADCLIFFE OP

You would expect a book called *The Dominican Way* to tell you about a particular Dominican way to God. The Benedictines follow their Rule, and the Jesuits practise the Ignatian Exercises, and so you might imagine that this would be a book about Dominican spirituality. But you will discover that the people you encounter in this book live very different lives. There is a painter, a scientist, a lawyer, writers, people involved in dialogue with Islam, a musician, teachers, contemplatives, and so on. Also, they seem to be strong personalities who would vigorously disagree with each other about almost everything! So, what makes them all Dominicans?

The official title of the Dominicans is the Order of Preachers. Preachers must discover their own voice and their own way of being, otherwise they will not speak authentically. Some of these Dominicans preach through art, others through writing or speaking, or by working for justice, or just by the silence of the monastic life. But all of them have authority because they speak as themselves, as the gifted, vulnerable, particular people they are. God's joy and beauty must reverberate through their particular flesh and blood humanity. We believe that our God became human, and so we must become human too if we are to speak well of God. In this book, you will meet men and women who are obviously human, passionate about different things, but alive! Dominic wished us to have the space to be ourselves, otherwise we could not speak of the God who has created each of us and wishes us to flourish.

The Dominicans are very democratic. We elect everyone who is in a major position of responsibility. St Dominic, our thirteenth-century founder, believed in democracy because everyone is given something to say, and so, if we are to find the right way forward as a community, we must listen to everyone, and there

1

is no point in doing this unless everyone has the courage and freedom to say what he or she *really* believes. Although the people here are very diverse, they all share a freedom to speak, a courage and joy in their lives and in God. Today in the Church, this is urgently needed!

There are interviews with nine men and eight women. This balance is not by accident, and for two reasons. First of all, the Church urgently needs the preaching of women if we are to be convincing. Secondly the Dominicans have been a family of men and women from the beginning. It is often imagined that members of religious orders are likely to be nervous of people of the other sex, regarding them as a temptation to be avoided, a threat to our celibacy! But from the earliest days, a natural, relaxed friendship between men and women was part of our tradition. St Dominic obviously enjoyed the company of women. His first community consisted of women, and he liked to return after his preaching to enjoy their company and encouragement. When he was dying, he confessed to preferring to talk to young women rather than being talked at by old women!

There was also the beautiful friendship between Jordan of Saxony, the second Master of the Order, and Blessed Diana, who wrote moving love letters to each other, and between St Catherine of Siena and Raymond of Capua. St Thomas Aquinas said that grace perfects nature, and God's grace blesses these natural friendships with people of the opposite sex.

Indeed friendship is part of our Dominican way. In some orders, the young were warned against 'particular friendships'. One must try to love everyone equally and have no favourites. But as a young friar, I was taught that the greater danger was to have particular enemies! We become loving people, able to talk about the God who is love, because we have learned to love in particular. Friendship nourishes our mission because we preach the eternal, equal friendship that is the very life of God.

This is a book of conversations, most of which took place in 2010, and we all found it enjoyable talking to Lucette Verboven! Preachers are often seen as people who address people from on high, beyond the risk of being challenged. But all good preaching springs from conversation. We love the fact that St Dominic founded the order in a pub! All night long he argued with the innkeeper, an Albigensian whose religion denied the goodness of creation. The innkeeper was converted, but a good conversation implies that you not only share your faith but that you listen to the other person, and are open to what he or she can teach you. We only have authority if we recognize the authority of the people with whom we talk.

In the Church today, we need much more conversation, especially with the young. It is only when we talk and listen that we can find how to offer a word that gives life and hope, a word that is spoken by the person that I am and respects who the other person is.

Wisely, Lucette did not want this book to be too long, but rather the sort of book that one can read easily wherever one is; relaxing on holiday or travelling. There were many more people whom she would love to have interviewed, but there was not space. I am a bit embarrassed that there are so many pages given to interviews with me, but any attempts to reduce these were firmly rebuffed!

Naturally, she often chose people who would arouse our interest because they were doing something unusual, such as a sister who is a university scientist, a Japanese brother who founded a Christian-Buddhist ashram, and a lay Dominican who is a famous composer. Also, because of a limited travel budget, she could only interview people, apart from one, who live in Europe or who were visiting it from their bases across the world.

But there are tens of thousands of members of the Order, all over the world, who are equally Dominican but whose lives never hit the headlines: brothers and sisters who study or teach in schools, work in parishes, are chaplains in hospitals or prisons, are missionaries founding the Church in new places. These are just as 'Dominican' as the ones you will meet in these pages, and you will usually find in them the same passion for truth and compassion that you find here.

1

Timothy Radcliffe

Passionately in love with truth

Growing up as a child in an aristocratic milieu in South England, Timothy Radcliffe cherished wandering around the woods. As a young Dominican, he worked one night a week with the homeless. As a demonstrator, he climbed the barriers of airbases to protest against nuclear armaments. 'The state is a false god,' he says. 'The world market creates the illusion that everything is for sale. The problem is not that we don't believe any more; we believe too much. Too many silly things.'

Impassioned by truth, Timothy Radcliffe sought out the religious order that had *veritas* as its motto. Thirty-two years later he was chosen to be its Master. Nevertheless, he brushes the idea of importance aside. 'You are a brother, no more, no less. If I come home, I wash my socks myself.'

Home. That is the Santa Sabina Priory on the Aventine, one of the hills of Rome. From his window, he can see the Vatican and the Forum. But Radcliffe is not often at home. He regularly visits his Dominican brothers and sisters who work in difficult circumstances all over the world; to talk with them, to instil fresh heart in them, or to weep with them, as in the Rwandan hospital where hundreds of maimed children waited for help.

His travels are often exhausting, the sorrow of the people he visits hard to bear. One of his fellow brothers, Pierre Claverie, who devoted himself to the dialogue between Muslims and Christians, was murdered in Algeria. 'The dialogue nipped in the bud?' I ask him. 'No,' he replies. 'Thousands of Muslims came to his funeral. Even if you are killed, the battle is not lost. Dialogue is a struggle, by definition. But the difference is whether you fight to destroy the other or to understand him. When Jacob fought with the angel, he was wounded but he was blessed at the same time.'

As we walk through the sunlit Roman cloister of the Santa Sabina, he tells me about the goal he has set himself: 'To meet all my brothers and sisters worldwide and give them time to speak what is in their minds and hearts.' An ambitious task! And he continues, 'We have to be messengers of hope and radiate this hope because the Gospel says that your life doesn't have to end in a blind alley. God always opens a way forward.'

> Timothy Radcliffe was born in London in 1945. He was educated at Oxford and Paris, taught theology at Oxford and was involved in ministry to the homeless and people with AIDS. He was Provincial of the English Province of the Order. As Master of the Order, he travelled widely in Asia, Africa and Latin America. He has gained an international reputation thanks to his thorough analysis of contemporary society and religion.

MEMORIES

What is your most precious childhood memory?

Something very important in my childhood was living in the countryside. I grew up in the woods and fields of southern England, very close to nature, to birds and animals. In my mind, the most wonderful education you can have is being in the countryside where you learn how to listen, how to look, how to walk through a wood without making a noise and be in touch with what's going on.

The first time I left that world was when I got a job before going to university and I began to make non-Catholic friends. For the first time in my life I had to ask, 'Is what I believe true?' And the question of truth became passionate for me. I remembered that there was a religious order with the motto *veritas*, 'truth', but I couldn't remember which it was, so I telephoned friends and eventually I found that it was the Dominican Order.

How old were you?

I was about 20. I turned up and told the Dominicans I wanted to join them.

Just like that? Because you had heard there was an order that was interested in truth?

(Laughing) That's right, yes! It was very impulsive.

When did you discover that the world was not as beautiful a place as you had thought it was?

As a young Dominican, I worked with the homeless one night a week. We ran a hostel where homeless people could come and sleep, eat and talk. I made inedible soup and discovered the humanity of people who lived on the street. In our society, these are the people who are often invisible – the people you walk around, the people you don't want to see – but they taught me to see their goodness, their humanity, their dignity. I remember my first Christmas after I became a Dominican. I was invited to the family of a fellow Dominican in Liverpool. There were nine children and their parents living in a small house. When they were young, lots of the children had to sleep in one bed. I was brusquely confronted with an England that I had never known and I was quite shocked.

What does study mean to you?

Study, all good study, is learning to be attentive, learning to listen. If study teaches you to be receptive to authors who are often dead, it should help you to be receptive to human beings who are alive.

The first successor as Master of the Order, Jordan of Saxony, said, 'Dominic understood all things through the humility of his heart.' I think that anybody who is not only interested in gathering facts but also in growing in wisdom, always has to question his own way of seeing the world. Opening your heart and mind to different ways of being a human, is necessary and liberating.

The joy of studying is discovering that you are wrong! It means being pushed beyond the limits of what you knew. I am

never so happy as when my favourite theories are destroyed...
well, in theory!

*Religion is often associated with a certain kind of morality that
we dislike.*

Morality is doing what you most deeply wish to do. Thomas
Aquinas said that people are fundamentally good and seek the
goodness that is God. It goes wrong when we allow ourselves
to be captured by small desires that cannot satisfy us. D. H.
Lawrence put it thus: 'The business of our Chief Thinkers is
to tell us of our deepest desires, not to keep shrilling our little
desires into our ears' (*A Propos of Lady Chatterley's Lover*).
Teaching a moral vision doesn't mean going around telling
people what is allowed and what is forbidden. It is inviting
people to discover the light of the Gospels, their fundamental
hunger for the good.

MASTER AND BROTHER

*In 1992, you were the first Englishman to be elected Master of
the Order of the Dominicans. What was your reaction?*

It was a complete surprise to me, I didn't even have the time to
think. My brothers asked me to do something and I said yes.

The word 'master' sounds very grand, but Dominic chose the
title because he did not want to be an abbot. Master originally
means 'teacher' and doesn't imply bossing people around. In
the Dominican Order, we are called friars or brothers and not
monks. The first thing you learn is that you are no more and no
less than a brother. When people arrive at Blackfriars, Oxford,
they sometimes ask us if we are a father or a brother, and, even
though we are ordained, we are taught to reply, 'I am a brother.'
I remember a visitor who saw a young man at the door cleaning
the floor. He asked, 'Are you a father or are you a brother?' The
young man said, 'I am a brother.' And the visitor said, 'Well,
brother, get me a cup of tea.' So he went and got a cup of tea.
Then the visitor said, 'Now, brother, take me to my room.' So he
took the visitor to his room. And the visitor said, 'Now, brother,
I wish to meet father prior.' And he said, 'I am the prior!'

Fundamental to being a Dominican is that you are just a brother, nothing more or less. And the brothers will never let you imagine that you are anything else! *(Laughs)*

What is your life like as a Master of the Order?

I travel a lot. In the first year, I visited some 20 countries, and then I stopped counting. I visit the brothers, sisters and lay people to see what they are doing and what I can do for them. It is my special task to visit the Dominicans who are living in circumstances of violence and poverty and to support and encourage them. That is why I have been so often to Rwanda, Burundi and the Congo.

What does such a visit imply?

The main thing is to speak individually to every brother; a meeting of about 30 minutes. Worldwide, I am responsible for some 6,500 brothers and 4,000 contemplative nuns. There are also about 36,000 active Dominican sisters in 176 different congregations who are part of the Dominican family, and perhaps 200,000 lay Dominicans of various sorts. Besides meeting the brethren one by one, I meet the community as a whole to discuss the challenges they face. The idea is not for me to come up with the answers or to take decisions for them, but to support them as they take responsibility for their lives and mission. If something is not working, then why?

I WEPT AT THE PITY OF IT

What has moved you most since your election as a Master?

The most powerful moment was the day I spent in Rwanda, at the beginning of the massacres in 1994, when we drove to the north to visit the Dominican sisters working in the refugee camps. We went to a brick-wall prison where there were 500 people packed inside.

But the worst thing was the hospital where the wards were filled with hundreds of children who had had arms and legs blown or cut off. I remember a boy who had lost both his legs, one of his arms and an eye. His father was sitting on the bed, weeping.

On the way there we had been stopped several times by groups of armed people who were waving their swords and guns, and I wondered whether we would ever arrive at our destination. Faced with the violence, faced with these mutilated children, what could I say? I remember that I left the hospital and just went out into the fields and wept. I wept at the pity of it.

When I went to the sisters, I could not think of anything I could say. But there was something we could do: celebrate Eucharist. We could remember a man who had faced his own death, gathered his friends and given himself to them. In the face of something so awful we are pushed beyond the limits of words. Sometimes gestures speak more than words, and so we repeat what Jesus did in the face of death, which carries the hope of resurrection.

ANY GOD THEY CAN FIND

The word 'God' is disappearing in our language. Is that a problem?

When people cease to worship the living God who liberates people, they worship any god they can find. I think the problem with our society is not that it has become secularized or that it is not interested in religion. In some ways we are far too religious, we worship far too many gods.

For example?

The state! You can see that this century has been crucified by the worship of state power, the worship of blood, the whole Arian mythology of Nazism. People were worshipping a false god. At the moment the ideology of the global market is reigning. But that is a false god. It seems to me that the role of the Church is not to invite people to believe; because everybody believes – but they believe crazy things; they believe in fate, in the stars, in horoscopes. What we have to do is to discover belief in the God who will liberate us from slavery. Most false gods demand we bow and worship. But our God tells us to stand up and be free. The revelation of the true God came when Moses led the people out of slavery in Egypt to meet God in the wilderness: the God who said, 'I am who I am.' He is the God who would set His people free.

What is your opinion of contemporary society?

A characteristic of our consumer culture is to think that everything is for sale. I talked about my childhood and the love of nature, the love of being in the woods and discovering animals, the sensation of living in a world that nobody can really own. Our ancestors knew that we can't really own the land, you can't own the seasons, the rain or fertility. But our culture is founded on what has been called by the Polish philosopher Leszek Kolakowski 'the commodity fiction' – that anything can be bought and sold. It ultimately means that we ourselves are for sale.

The great enslavement of Africans beginning in the seventeenth century, turning them into commodities to be exported, like cattle, to America, was symptomatic of a deep crisis which touched every country in the West. Putting people on the labour market where they must sell themselves seems to be a part of the cultural crisis of our times. If we see everything as for sale, how can we be aware of the God who is the giver of all good things?

TRUTH-TELLING

What is the most urgent problem faced by our present-day society?

Violence. I think that the competitive, individualistic, ruthless society in which we live, the society of the market, is violent. It does violence to us. It is reflected in all the pain of broken-down families, the destruction of community.

I have just been to South Africa and seen a society which suffers terrible wounds: murders committed by the very highest members of the government. The Truth and Reconciliation Commission has the role of trying to build a future by bringing to light what happened. Truth-telling can easily look like accusation, but it is very different, because truth-telling heals a community whereas accusation places a burden on someone. The difference is beautifully illustrated by the poem 'A Poison Tree' by William Blake, which begins:

> I was angry with my friend:
> I told my wrath, my wrath did end.
> I was angry with my foe;
> I told him not, my wrath did grow.

The first is a healing process; the second is a condemnation.

RELIGION IS NOT RELEVANT

What role do you see for religion and the Church in the twenty-first century?

Putting the question that way confirms the impression that religion is somehow intended to be relevant. But I don't think religion is relevant at all. Faith discloses that to which everything else is relevant. Anything only has relevance in so much as it belongs to our journey to God. God is not relevant. To try to make religion relevant is to try to use God for little purposes, as if God were a fitness trainer or bank manager. But ultimately that is a blasphemy.

There seems to be a hierarchical Church, which is rather authoritarian, and another one, close to ordinary people. Are there two Churches or is there just one?

Every human society needs structure. You can't have a football game unless you have a structure: not everybody will be a striker, not everybody can be keeping goal. You can't have music unless the orchestra has a structure. But what matters is that the structure, which you could call a hierarchy, empowers people and is not there to dominate them. This does usually happen, but not always. Sometimes you find places where you feel that it is not working and that the experiences of women and of lay people, for example, are not heard. But that's not because it is a hierarchy; it is because the hierarchy is not working to empower them.

We live in a highly individualistic society which is deeply suspicious of structure. But if we succumb to that individualism, I think more people will be hurt and excluded. Our job in the Church is to become strong together.

THREATENED TO BE KILLED

What if people are intentionally dishonest and don't want dialogue?

Well, you can't get very far then. But most people do want dialogue. I suppose the biggest challenge at the moment is dialogue with Islam. It is one of the main priorities of the Order. We have institutes for dialogue with Islam in many places: Multan in Pakistan, Cairo, Istanbul and so on. Sometimes there is a wonderful openness – we are all children of Abraham – but sometimes there isn't. One of our brothers, Pierre Claverie, who was the Bishop of Oran in Algeria, gave all his life to seeking dialogue with Islam. And one day, 1 August 1996, he was assassinated by a bomb. An anti-tank bomb had been built into the side of his house and was detonated as he went back home. It killed him and his young Muslim driver.

So, the dialogue was nipped in the bud?

Many people said, 'This is a sign of the impossibility of dialogue.' But at his funeral three days later, which I attended, there were thousands of Muslims, and the final testimony was from a young woman who said, 'He was the Bishop of the Muslims. He brought us back to faith. We believe in Allah because of him.' It was a wonderful example of how, even when you are frustrated, even when you seem to make no progress, even when they threaten to kill you, you should never give up.

Like Jacob wrestling with the angel, which left him wounded but blessed at the same time?

Any real dialogue with another person is bound to be a struggle. There is no interesting argument if there is not a disagreement. But it makes a difference whether you fight to destroy the other person or to understand him. True dialogue is a struggle to come to illumination. You are both drawn to a truth which is larger than either started with.

You say that it's not enough to retell the story of the resurrection, but that we need an initiation in the experience as well. What do you mean?

The resurrection happens today. Let me give you an example of a Dominican sister I know. She works in the village of Kawat in Gujurat, India. When she arrived in this village, she found the people utterly impoverished. They were all in the hands of moneylenders: in order to buy seeds to plant the fields, they had to borrow money and they could never make enough money from their crops to escape the debt. They lived as if they were imprisoned. That sister set up a little Dominican bank to lend money at almost no interest, so that the villagers could sell their crops, build their farms, make their homes and come alive. It's a little resurrection.

Every human being will have to go through little moments of death and resurrection. You may need to meet death and resurrection in your own life, or you can see it happen in the life of a society. I have seen extraordinary moments of resurrection in South Africa after apartheid. From all these situations, perhaps you learn to listen anew to the story of the man who died and rose again. The death and resurrection of Jesus is obviously infinitely more than that – it really is a triumph over death. But when we defeat the powers of death in society and in our own lives, we may begin to understand.

ALL THESE IMPORTANT PEOPLE

There are many pictures of your predecessors on this wall. Will your picture hang here one day?

I suppose that's inescapable. But I shall wait until the last possible minute before the picture goes up! When I arrived here, I walked down this corridor and saw all these paintings, and my heart dropped. All these important people, all these famous names! It was a very depressing first ten minutes, and then I discovered the wonderful liberty of realizing that I don't know who most of these people are. Most of these earlier Masters did what they had to do and were forgotten. And that will be the same for me. Thanks to God.

2

Jean-Jacques Pérennès

Go where things are difficult!

'One of our friars in Iraq had his name written on the wall of the monastery, together with the message: "You are the next one to be killed."' Jean-Jacques Pérennès, Vicar Provincial of the Dominicans in the Arab countries, is monitoring the situation closely. 'Twenty years ago there were 1.5 million Christians living in Iraq. Now their number is estimated at only 400,000.'

Nevertheless, on this last Saturday of August – the feast day of St Augustine – six young friars, including three from Iraq, are pronouncing their solemn vows in the packed monastery church in Lille. Their families, many of whom have had to endure violence, are present.

But today the sorrow stays in the background. The beautifully decorated church is watching and waiting as the young friars fall prostrate on the ground and Brother Bruno Cadoré, the Provincial of France who is now the Master of the Order, asks, 'What do you want?' When the answer comes, 'God's mercy and yours,' he calls the friars before him one by one. He listens to their vows and embraces them in a tender, fatherly way. High-pitched Christian-Arab voices acclaim the words of Samer, Cyrille-Marie, Christian-Marie, Adrien, Zeyad, Nouiran: 'I, brother Samer, make profession and vow obedience...'

Afterwards, there is wine and pasta in the sunny courtyard of the monastery, to which I am kindly invited. As I am joined by a young Egyptian friar, I notice the profound joy he shares with his newly professed brothers.

Joy is also a key word in the life of another Dominican friar, Pierre Claverie, who completed his novitiate in this priory some

50 years ago and who was assassinated in Algeria. But if the stones of this church in Lille could speak, they would echo the final words of Claverie's solemn profession: '...and I vow obedience to the rule of St Augustine, the Dominican Preachers and the Master of the Order until I die.'

Jean-Jacques Pérennès was born in 1949 in Tréguier, France to a family with a strong Christian background. He studied philosophy, economics and theology in Lyon and Paris. He lived in Algeria for ten years, during which time he spent a year with Pierre Claverie, the future Bishop of Oran, whose biography he later wrote. As a promoter of justice and peace for the Order and a close collaborator of Timothy Radcliffe, then Master of the Order, he travelled widely. He has been working for 11 years at IDEO, the Dominican Institute for Oriental Studies in Cairo founded by Georges Anawati, whose biography Pérennès has also written.

EVERYBODY LEFT

Why did you want to become a Dominican?

After Vatican II, there were many challenging discussions in the Church. When I came across a magazine called *Signes des temps* published by Les Editions du Cerf and found out that the publishers were Dominicans, I contacted them. It took me just a few weeks to decide to join the Order. I was only 18 at the time.

You studied during tumultuous times. How were you affected?

Events in France in May 1968 produced a big shock within the Church and the Order. We were nine in my novitiate and, within four years, everybody left except me. Even the master of the novices got married later! During my military service I volunteered to go to Algeria as a teacher and met Pierre Claverie. My life was in crisis, as I had fallen in love and had also thought about leaving. Pierre and the small, joyful community in Algeria, that had real challenges to live up to, provided answers to my questions.

What did you learn from him?

His happiness and commitment. It took me years to understand his story. Only in writing his biography did I discover important elements of his life, such as his upbringing. His parents had had a tough childhood, so they wanted to found a loving family. I think that's where his maturity stemmed from; that and his intellectual life and prayer. Pierre was not somebody who shared intimately about himself, but he was very authentic.

I was on my way to a congress of young Dominicans in Spain with Timothy Radcliffe when I learned of his assassination. At the airport in Madrid, struggling to get a ticket to Algeria, I experienced my most difficult moments. As his murder hit the headlines, I saw his picture in the newspapers that people in the ticket queue were reading. I was devastated.

How did writing Claverie's biography affect you?

Pierre's death contributed to a kind of burnout I experienced. The end of my term in the Santa Sabina with Timothy Radcliffe was nearing and I was very tired. A friend of mine had suggested that I write Claverie's biography but I didn't have the strength. I took a year's sabbatical and then one day I started writing his story and I just didn't stop. It was like giving birth.

Writing his biography was profoundly healing. To this day, I am impressed by the echo of his life. I have given some hundred or so lectures about him in Africa, Europe and the Middle East. Pierre Claverie's story continues to be very meaningful because it is about reaching 'the other'. A team of friars is preparing to read texts of his at the Festival of Avignon. This echo in secular France, 15 years after his death, is just amazing!

L'ACADEMIE DE LA BIERE

You worked closely with Timothy Radcliffe in Rome when he was Master of the Order. What was it like?

We had been students together in Paris. I studied economics, as I was interested in Third World projects, and Timothy, who was at the Convent Saint Jacques, studied philosophy. We used to go to L'Académie de la bière – a pub on Boulevard Arago – and had a lot of interesting discussions. When, much later, Timothy was elected Master of the Order during the Mexico Chapter in 1992, he asked me to join him. He put together a team of amazing diversity and communicated his enthusiasm and freedom. I remember the very early intuition he had about the internet as a place of preaching. Today it has become evident. Timothy has this grace of new ideas and he is very free.

When you are elected to such an important position, people often think you have to adjust to the people in power. Timothy enjoyed good relationships with the Vatican, but he was not submissive. He was a friar, a preacher, a theologian, and he travelled around the world to help the brothers. In some ways his theology is quite traditional – he studied Thomas Aquinas – but he has the capacity to reach people on the margins. On our first trip together, just after his election, we spent seven weeks in Africa, visiting Benin, Nigeria, Kenya, Rwanda, Burundi, Angola, Cameroon and Zaire.

What was most poignant during these voyages?

Rwanda was very difficult. I remember travelling to a hospital with Timothy where children had had their legs or arms cut off. Terrible! In addition to that, no material comfort whatsoever was available, not even sheets on the beds.

As a promoter of justice and peace, I also frequently visited the refugee camps of Haiti and Pakistan. I remember the desolation of Lithuania, Ukraine, Albania. But at the same time we felt it of great importance to be there.

What difference can you make?

An enormous one! If the Church is not present where things are difficult, it does not make sense to go there when it is easy. Moreover, our presence is very much appreciated. I am sometimes asked, 'What can you do?' But it is not a matter of *doing* in the first place. You have to *be* with people in need. Sometimes I can only express my grief.

Is compassion enough to make up for the suffering?

Priests attending to prostitutes, for example, can't do much against the pimps, but they can offer a cup of tea and listen. Compassion is a very important element of Dominican life. It is said that Saint Dominic was moved to tears by human suffering. We, too, need to cultivate this sensitivity!

In Brazil, Henri Burin des Roziers has a price on his head. In Algeria, Pierre Claverie was killed. Is a vocation worth risking your life for?

The case of Henri Burin des Roziers is an extreme one. He is a very committed lawyer; he will never give up. He is 80, unwell and tired, but he keeps promoting the cases of the landless people against the big landowners. He has a £30,000 bounty on his head, but he won't be stopped.

Pierre Claverie in Algeria is a similar example. I think there are two reasons to continue our work in the Arab world. Firstly, we shouldn't fail the Christians who are living in these countries, especially the ones who are too poor to leave. Secondly, the Arab world needs bridge-builders between Christians and Muslims. One of our friars has recently completed a PhD on the Shia. He went for his research to Nadjaf and Karbala in his white Dominican habit and was well received.

In his habit?

Yes. Most Muslims are not extremists and accept us!

But do they want to maintain relationships with Christians?

Many people do. When there is no freedom for Christians, rules get tighter for Muslims as well.

How can you preach in the Muslim world when it is not allowed?

Chris McVey, an American Dominican who spent most of his life in Pakistan, used the phrase 'to meet God out of the camp', as is quoted in Exodus. We have to reach 'the other', but at the same time we are like St Dominic *in medio ecclesiae*, 'in the middle of the Church'. So I am not freelance; I'm sent by the community to preach in the name of the Church and the Order.

*In the Middle East, no churches may be built, in contrast to the
building of mosques in the West.*

There is only one country where churches can't be built: Saudi
Arabia, and that is because of the presence there of two holy
places, Mecca and Medina. Many Christians from the Far East
who work there – Filipinos, Indians and Pakistanis – must
worship in secret, it's true. But in the other countries of the
Middle East – Qatar, Dubai, Abu Dhabi, Kuwait, Yemen –
churches are open. All worshippers are foreigners indeed, but
there's no prohibition against attending Mass. Last year I said
Mass in Qatar on a Friday. It was one of the 12 Masses of the
day and 2,700 people attended!

It is true, however, that in Egypt and Iraq, the situation has
become more difficult for Christians because of fanatical groups
and the spreading of an atmosphere of intolerance among
Muslims.

A WOUNDED MEMORY

*The Dominican Institute of Oriental Studies in Cairo is an
ambitious project. What is its goal?*

It was started in the 1950s by Father Anawati, an Egyptian
Dominican who was a specialist in the history of Arabic
philosophy. He recognized that it was difficult to engage with
Muslims on a religious level, but he looked for other possibilities. He established IDEO with the aim of trying to develop a
relationship with the Muslim intelligentsia on the level of studies
and culture. As a result, we have established one of the main
libraries in Islamic studies in the Middle East.

Bigger than the one in Alexandria?

Better! Alexandria has pieces of everything. We have a corpus
of the most important material in Islamic studies in Arabic and
western languages as well, which is very unusual in the Middle
East. It has about 140,000 books and many magazines, journals
and reviews. For Muslims who want to study their own tradition
or the Christian tradition, it's a very important resource.

Do Muslims come to a Dominican library?

They most certainly do. Sometimes veiled women and men with heavy beards use our library to study. Some are even looking for texts of St Augustine or Thomas Aquinas. They appreciate our library, we don't charge, we are kind to them and we respect Islam. There is a discreet place for prayer near the library with small carpets.

Pierre Claverie used to say that before we can have dialogue, we need common words. Muslims and Christians share a wounded memory. Many Muslims want to study the crusades, which is one of their big wounds. Our task is to meet 'the other' and to show Muslims that we can build relationships without trying to convert them. Helping them in their studies is a start.

When I published my book on Georges Anawati, I asked a very distinguished Muslim lady, Mrs Zeinab El-Khodeiry, to write the preface. She is a former dean of the faculty of philosophy at Cairo University. People like her are much more than a bridge, as are several imams who visit our library and with whom we have become friends.

But how can you establish relationships when women are not allowed to show their faces or to shake hands?

An educated person like Mrs El-Khodeiry is not veiled and has no problems with shaking hands. The veil is an obligation for strict Muslims. We oversimplify things in the West. One of our Muslim employees, for example, was not veiled, and then one day she turned up to work with a veil. It seemed that she had to look respectable in order to be able to get married. Later, she stopped wearing the veil, which shows that customs can vary in Muslim society.

The newly appointed Grand Imam of Al Azhar for the Sunnis in Cairo praised the Dominicans in Egypt for their work. Is that a recognition that can count?

Yes, that's absolutely amazing. Dr Ahmed al Tayeb studied philosophy at the Sorbonne. He is a Sufi, which means that he has a background in spiritual Islam. When he gave his first interview and was asked how it was possible for a Grand Imam to have studied in Paris, he reproached the journalist for forgetting that in the past many Egyptians were scholars and that imams had been trained in major cities in the West. He added, 'Go to the Dominican library and see how much these people respect the Muslim culture.' It was a wonderful endorsement. It means that our work is valued by scholars. It is political Islam that poses problems, and our brother Emilio Platti has specialized in that.

Is Islam compatible with modernity?

It is a big issue and a very old one. During the first centuries of Islam, a lot of philosophers went very far in their debate on faith and rationality. But this *Mutazili* movement became blocked. During the nineteenth century, the Grand Imam Muhammad Abduh made a strong effort in Egypt to try to create an Arab renaissance – *Nahda* – but failed.

Political analysts suspect that Muslim fundamentalism could stem from a fear of modernity. Look at the skyline of Cairo and see that two things are prominent: minarets and television antennae, all shouting to see who is strongest! Imams try to convince the people of the importance of religion, but at the same time the kids want to wear jeans, go to McDonald's and listen to pop music.

AN OLD IDEA

For how long have Dominicans been present in the Middle East?

In the thirteenth century, Ricoldo of Monte Croce was the first Dominican to go to Baghdad, where he stayed for ten years, learned Arabic and became familiar with the court of the Mongol Il-Khan ruler Arghun. He was often homesick for his native town, Florence, but he was determined to establish a Dominican presence in a Muslim place. Our first priory in Istanbul also dates back to the late thirteenth century. That building has since become a mosque and we have had to look for new premises, but we are still present, which is wonderful.

Why must Christianity be present in Muslim countries?

In Ricoldo's time, conversion was the goal, so the Dominicans established language schools in Tunis where the friars could study Arabic. Nowadays our goal is to be witnesses to the Gospel and to support Christians who are still living there. We are very careful not to proselytize because a Muslim is not free to change religion.

He can be killed.

Socially threatened to say the least. Or he may have to leave his country and lose everything. I hope that this is a temporary situation. Don't forget that all these tensions only started in the late 1970s with the Iranian revolution and the invasion of Afghanistan by the Russians. When the Wahhabis from Saudi Arabia started to pour money and propaganda into the Arab countries, it became worse.

How did the idea for a Dominican presence in Arab countries come about?

It's an old idea from the Dominican Order and the Holy See. In the late 1930s, an evaluation of one century of mission was made. It turned out that this nineteenth-century mission had been unsuccessful in Muslim countries. So, instead of the traditional missions, the idea grew to try to build a confident relationship with Muslims. It was from this that the Dominican friar Georges Anawati laid the foundations of the IDEO. Anawati had two tools: knowledge and friendship. He stressed that we need to be well-informed about Islam's historical and cultural achievements. And at the same time it is important to build human relationships. I have very good Muslim friends, and I know that our friendship runs so deep that we can have arguments because we will have tea again afterwards.

GIVING AWAY HIS LIFE

You have given examples of the good relationships Christians and Muslims can enjoy with each other, but ultimately, Pierre Claverie was assassinated!

First of all, we don't know exactly who killed him. It's a big issue. The situation in Algeria was very confused. The last time

I met Pierre, I had an feeling of foreboding because he spoke so openly in the media. If he had kept a lower profile, he might still have been alive. But keeping silent wouldn't have made sense for him. In speaking out, he was also a kind of advocate for the Muslims who were fighting for an open society. Humanité plurielle, 'Plural humanity', is his last text. In it he said, 'We need windows, we need perspective.'

He was assassinated in Oran on 1 August 1996. It is striking that he was killed at the entrance to his chapel: the same place where he prayed. When we prepared for the tenth anniversary of his death, the situation was still difficult in Algeria. As we didn't know how many people would join us, we had arranged a simple celebration at night and a Mass the following day. We started with 50 attendees, but in the end 400 came! Imagine that number of people, mainly Muslims, coming to honour the memory of a bishop who had been killed ten years ago!

What does that mean?

On the one hand, his death was an enormous loss, but, on the other hand, it shows that in some situations it makes sense to give everything. It was not his choice to be a martyr. On the contrary, he was very Mediterranean: he liked food and enjoyed the company of friends! His spiritual life ran very deep, although he was discreet about it.

After his death, I was asked to collect his personal belongings. His pyjamas, his books... everything could be put in two small bags! His room was more modest than those of many friars. In some ways he had been giving away his life for years. His door was always open to everybody. He gave generously of his time. During the last weeks of his life, he had been writing about Dietrich Bonhoeffer who had fought Nazism. He felt close to him as he recognized the same fight.

You write that Claverie enjoyed the freedom that came from his Dominican training. In what way does the Order encourage freedom? Is it the freedom to come and go as you please?

Not at all. We enjoy freedom, but at the same time we make a vow of obedience and sometimes we are sent to places where we are unwilling to go. There are many different kinds of

Dominicans. You met Oshida in Japan: a completely free spirit and yet a profound Dominican!

We are a big family, used to welcoming different people. Some are very traditional, some are a bit crazy! But if you stop talking to one another, you have a problem. During Mass today, you saw that our friars are very different in style! The intellectual life is also very important for freedom. If you take studying seriously, you don't know where it will lead you. Some Dominicans became Marxists during their studies and left the priesthood.

Freedom is linked to obedience, which may seem a paradox. My former university colleagues are pursuing careers while I don't know where I'll be sent next. But this holds many advantages as well. I would never have imagined working in Egypt or getting involved with Iraqis. It's a wonderful task. It was not my choice; I just said yes when I was asked.

What does prayer mean to you?

I am not very good at prayer, but at least it gives me a pause in my very active life. Muslims have their five moments of prayer and they respect that absolutely. Thanks to them, when the bell rings to announce our prayer times, I can ask my visitors to come back in 15 minutes!

Are you still happy being a Dominican?

Extremely. I fell in love with the Order at a very young age. It was totally irrational but it has enriched my life tremendously.

Which Dominicans were a source of inspiration to you?

Dominic is certainly very meaningful because of his compassion and his desire to talk with people. His night with the heretic Albigensians in Montpellier has become famous. I like his courage for sending the friars two-by-two to Bologna, to Madrid, to different cities. People told him it was too early, but he just said, 'I know what I am doing.' And he was right.

Thomas Aquinas, too, is very interesting. During the Middle Ages, when everything was in turmoil, he put together a new philosophy and theology. Bartolomé de Las Casas was a colonial and discovered the Gospel through the lives of the slaves; he converted. And from time to time you have people like Pierre Claverie and Henri Dominique Lacordaire, the French Dominican who re-established the Order in France in the nineteenth century, after it had been suppressed by the French Revolution.

THREATS

What is the situation in Iraq for the friars?

Nobody regrets the removal of Saddam, but he was able to keep a very diverse country together: the Shi'as, the Sunnis, the Kurds, the Christians. Extremist Islam has made the situation disastrous for Christians. Twenty years ago, there were 1.5 million Christians, now their number is estimated at only 400,000.

Have the Dominicans in Baghdad and Mosul received any threats?

We have had to pay money to avoid kidnappings, yes. Some friars have had death threats, but even so, they have chosen to stay, which is very courageous. But these friars are Iraqis. It is their country. Christianity is their religion.

Who would want to become a Dominican in troubled countries like these?

Three young Iraqi friars pronounced their solemn vows today and two novices are entering the noviciate next month. We are small and fragile, but present, by the grace of God!

3

James MacMillan

I have a sound of God

A fierce, provocative Scot? James MacMillan laughs at the idea and waves it away as a caricature of the mad, whisky-drinking Scottish highlander shaking his fist at the world. 'No', he says. 'I'm a very relaxed person.' Nevertheless, he has built a reputation of not being afraid to speak out on a variety of subjects. He considers Scotland's anti-Catholic sectarianism to be a wound that has marred society and can be healed only by first opening it up. So he did, by making a speech at the Edinburgh Festival in 1999. And was showered with criticism afterwards. Looking back on that episode, he reflects, 'I have been demonized in Scotland, but my criticism has been effective. Scottish society has engaged with this issue since.'

Another row arose around his liturgical settings for the papal Masses when Pope Benedict XVI visited the UK in September 2010. 'The old guard of liturgical trendies attempted to boycott me. It's all water under the bridge now. The visit was a huge success.' MacMillan seems to thrive on confrontations and unorthodox behaviour. When he was a student, he took part in communist meetings, but occasionally left them to go to Mass, which drew down eyebrows. As a composer, he is much in favour for reintroducing Gregorian chant, while his interest in liberation theology made him record *Cantos Sagrados* as a protest against the repression in Latin America. At a time when liberals and conservatives take opposite stands, his side is 'making music for God'. His whole life has been a preparation for this, so he says. It sounds like the confession of a medieval monk. Yet MacMillan is an unashamed modernist and a lay Dominican.

29

The London hotel room where we meet has a gorgeous view overlooking Lambeth Palace. This causes MacMillan to muse about his collaboration with a younger Rowan Williams, who is now living in this beautiful yellow palace as the Archbishop of Canterbury. They had a fruitful cooperation, leading to MacMillan's creation of the musical piece *Parthenogenesis*, filled with meditative and turbulent moments. Music filled with contrasts, like the composer himself.

James MacMillan was born in 1959 in Kilwinning, Scotland. He is an internationally renowned composer and conductor. His operas, concertos, symphonies, sacred music and many orchestral and instrumental works are influenced by his Roman Catholic faith and his Scottish heritage. His specially commissioned congregational Mass was performed when Pope Benedict XVI beatified Cardinal Newman during his visit to Britain in September 2010. He and his wife Lynne are lay Dominicans and live in Glasgow.

FROM DAY ONE

When did you first come into contact with music?

The most significant thing, as a child of about 8, was being given a little recorder while I was at school. It had a great impact on me, as it made me want to play instruments. From day one I wanted to write music, although I didn't know what that meant at the time. Just the physical experience of picking up an instrument and playing some notes on it generated something that has never left me.

The earliest musical memory that had an impact on me was being taken to the Catholic Cathedral in Edinburgh when I was 5 years old. I heard music from Tomás Luis de Victoria or Giovanni Pierluigi da Palestrina, composers of the sixteenth century. There was a mystery of something sacred going on and I think back on it as a seminal moment.

LAY DOMINICAN

What influenced you most when you were young?

I went to Edinburgh University and the chaplain at that time was a young Aidan Nichols, who has since become a very important theological figure in the English-speaking world and in the Dominican Order. Father Aidan married my wife and me a few years later. He opened up the world of Dominican charisms to me – the history of the Dominicans – and through him I came into contact with people like Timothy Radcliffe.

Why were you attracted to the Dominicans?

First and foremost, their scholarship; the fact that they invite people into a deeper intellectual understanding of their faith, and not in an elitist way because everyone is invited to consider more deeply what it means to be a Christian in the modern world. Sometimes that will involve study of the writings of the church fathers, the scriptures or other texts that will lead to a deeper reflection on the great traditions of the Church.

Through my involvement with the Dominicans I came to understand history and culture from the past, and this has influenced me as a composer and a Christian. I was always attracted by the people that I met in the Dominicans. Sometimes they were liberal people, sometimes they were traditionalists, but there was something that connected them and it goes right back to Dominic himself. Catherine of Siena is the patron of the lay Order and we have visited Siena on pilgrimage on a couple of occasions. Fra Angelico has a special attraction for me as he was a fellow artist. These people were of great, sometimes mysterious inspiration for me.

Do you remember the moment you became a lay Dominican? Did you pronounce a vow?

I have regarded myself as a lay Dominican since my student days, although there was nothing formal about it then. Nevertheless, I was part of an undergraduate 'drift' towards the Dominican Order in Edinburgh. I formally became a lay Dominican about ten years ago with my wife Lynne. There is a thriving Dominican presence in Glasgow, initially centred around the Catholic chaplaincy at Strathclyde University. We renew our vows every three years.

What are the effects of being a lay Dominican?

I feel close to the friars and the nuns, locally and universally. I feel plugged in to the workings of the Order; their traditions are now mine! We celebrate the major feast days of Dominican saints in a very real way. I am inspired to do more. Liturgical life needs to be developed, both for our little group locally in my parish of St Columba's and for the Order nationally. Some Dominicans have let liturgical life drift aimlessly, and this needs to be addressed. In that sense, we are no different from any other part of the Church, but the Order of Preachers has its own liturgical charisms from tradition which need to be reawakened. Some places, like Blackfriars in Cambridge and Oxford, are making strong and steady strides in this sphere, but we really need to be up to speed. What is the Church, after all, without its liturgy? Writing music is a form of preaching for me.

Is it important that your wife is a lay Dominican too? Do your children sometimes question you about it?

My wife Lynne and I are very close in our spiritual lives. The Dominicans brought her into the Church, baptized and confirmed her, and then married us. Our children talk to us all the time about it. They come to Mass with us, and my daughters sing in my choir on Sunday mornings. When they leave home soon, they will make their own way. I don't know whether the Dominicans will figure in their adult lives. We'll see...

You aren't afraid of outing yourself a Catholic. Aren't you afraid of losing commissions?

Christians are living in difficult times again. The fact that they succumb to a fear about even admitting that they are Christians points to something going wrong in our society. I have certainly noticed a growing militancy in anti-religious voices. Gone are the days of the 1970s when there used to be dialogue between people of faith and people who didn't share the faith. There is a new and aggressive fundamentalism in atheism now. People like Richard Dawkins even want to expel religion from public spaces.

A CARPENTER OF TIME

You speak of desecration cultivated by new ruling elites. Can you give examples?

In the Preamble of the Treaty of Lisbon in 2007, the Christian heritage is not even mentioned. But Christianity is a huge part of our culture as Europeans; more so than Mediterranean and Greek antiquity. This attempt to take out of the equation not only our historical memory, but also the very concept of what the sacred might mean is dangerous. Human beings throughout history have engaged with a sense of the sacred. As a musician, I recognize in music a continuous historical searching for a sense of 'the other' in our world. Humanity is at its best when it is making music and opening up to the potential of immaterial otherness. Modern capitalism has hoodwinked humanity and society into thinking that all we need is a house, a car, money, a materialistic life. But there is a constant and universal thirst for more than the sum of our parts; that's why religion is not dying.

What is music?

Good question. Is it just the notes on the pages? Is it just those static black symbols, those complicated visual patterns? In a sense that *is* all it is! But those static symbols don't really account for the sometimes convulsive impact that music has on our lives. What is essential is not just the immateriality of music but its numinous nature. Music is not physical – you can't see or touch it, you can't eat or drink it – yet its power reaches deep down into not just our psyche, but into the deep crevasses of the soul. It's that immateriality that makes us ask questions about the otherness of things and can open up our lives to being touched by powers that are not visible or physical. Music is a deep mystery in our lives, in our history and in our society. It's one of the great joys of being a human being.

Music is said to be an architecture of time. Composers shape a segment of time into a little drama. 'Time' is the material they work with. Are composers carpenters?

You can certainly call them carpenters of time, although music theologians like Messiaen, for example, looked beyond the confines of time to a kind of timelessness. It is interesting to see that music, which is so time-restricted, can nevertheless expand one's awareness of the reality of timelessness. In the same way, music exposes us to another concept of the divine, namely that God does not exist in time. I suppose that's where I agree with atheists, because there is no such thing as God. God is not a thing like me or you or this table, it's something beyond 'thingness'.

What is your image of God?

I have no image of God. I have a sound of God, because I'm a composer. I have sounds in my head which I think have something to do with God. These sounds are hard to put into words, but I try to capture that sonic imagination and bring it to life. I think composers are vessels of the divine, without being too arrogant about it. Composers have that glimpse, which is not a visual glimpse, but a spiritual glimpse through sound. For me, it's a sound that is, in essence, silenced; it only exists in the imagination of one's inner ear. The composer has to bring that to life almost as a kind of mirror image of the creation of the cosmos. We are mirrors of God, who is the creator of all. We are trying to mimic Him by giving space to His sonic image.

Do you dream about music?

I do, and I am not the only composer who does! In fact, I dream a lot about music-making. Even when one is unconscious, the process of making music is going on. Sometimes I tell young composers who are suffering from composer's block not to worry. Just because they aren't writing doesn't mean that the composition is not ongoing – it is going on 'underground', outside their consciousness. And it can surge up at the right moment, like a geyser from the earth.

Do you prepare yourself, with silence or prayer?

Sometimes I do and sometimes I don't. It is important, however, to find a preparatory silent time for reflection, silence, meditation, prayer. I pray with difficulty. We live in a time when it is very difficult to focus concentration on anything, let alone prayer. It is difficult to clear one's mind and soul of all the clutter in order to listen to a piece of music. When I pray, I use the prayer of the church; I love liturgy. Sometimes words can deflect me. Sometimes I'm very anxious about the best way to pray. Praying requires an emptying of oneself, an opening up. There is a musical analogy because in order to listen to music, you need to empty yourself. When you use music simply as background, you lose the essence of what music is. Listening to music has become a privilege in this day and age. It has nothing to do with class or education, money or breeding.

Perhaps. But you have to be educated in classical music before you can enjoy it!

One also has to be educated to be able to read, in order to understand everything.

Being able to read and write is a basic need, while going to concert halls isn't.

I think there's an analogy between reading and music. One wouldn't argue against basic education in reading, so I can't understand why one would argue against basic education in music. Psychiatrists and researchers have proved that openness to music affects the whole human, and makes one a more rounded and fulfilled person. This is something that Pythagoras and Plato could have told us. But we've lost the understanding of the meaning of music because our society is dominated by the verbal and the visual. Music has become a noise in the background. It may be a soundtrack to our lives, but it is mere background, never the core of our lives. If it were, it would change the nature of that core existence – it would beautify and sanctify it.

THREE DAYS

*In your compositions, you seem to focus on the three days
before Easter – Maundy Thursday, Good Friday and the Easter
Vigil. Why are you so passionate about it?*

I can't really account for that. But if one sees the resurrection
as the centrally important historical event in human history,
one can't really engage with it without understanding what
happened before. One has to engage with the suffering of Christ
through Good Friday in order to fully understand the vast impli-
cations of the resurrection. That's why I keep coming back to
it. My *Saint John Passion* is a visit to the sepulchre; *The Seven
Last Words from the Cross* is a kind of cantata that explores the
crucifixion; Visitatio Sepulchri is another visit to the sepulchre;
Fourteen Little Pictures deals with the fourteen stations of the
cross. But there's also *Triduum* which is a triptych. It starts with
the Thursday piece, *The World's Ransoming*. The Good Friday
piece is the cello concerto which I wrote for Rostropovich, who
also commissioned the third piece – the symphony, *Vigil*. All
three relate to the events and liturgies of the Easter Triduum.

Culturally, we know deep in our bones what the sepulchre
means. As human beings we confront death all the time, but
we're also asking profound questions about the meaning of life.
That's what artists do in many different ways. My way of asking
these questions is to confront the emptiness and darkness of the
tomb and the promise of life after death, whatever that means.

Do you believe that?

Yes, I do, because I feel drawn to reflect on it even though it
is a mystery. I haven't rejected it as so many people have, who
call it a fairy tale. In fact, Messiaen said that the Catholic faith
is one great fairy tale with the essential difference from other
fairy tales: it is all true. There is great wisdom in that. There is
a great delight in fairy tales; they appeal to the child in all of
us; and if a composer can't keep the child in him alive in his
adult years he wouldn't be a composer. If you can't keep your
child alive, especially as a person of faith, something essential
in you dies.

ROSTROPOVICH

You mentioned Mstislav Rostropovich. The images of him playing the cello in the besieged White House during the early days of Perestroika were spread worldwide. Did you know him well?

Yes, I became a friend. Later in his life, he conducted the American premiere of my percussion concerto *Veni Veni Emmanuel* in Washington in 1993. I went over for it and was astounded. I expected him to be distant and aloof, but he wasn't like that at all. He embraced me immediately, and he behaved as if he had always known me. He invited the percussionist Evelyn Glennie and myself to his apartment in Washington and he talked about his life and the musicians he had known, such as Shostakovich, Prokofiev, Benjamin Britten. He had stood in the presence of Stalin, Khrushchev and Brezhnev. His experience and understanding of Soviet history was amazing, but also terrifying in his narration of it. By the end of that evening he had invited me to write the cello concerto and *Vigil* symphony for him, and I left pinching myself, wondering what had happened.

On that night, he told an amazing story from when the new democracy was under attack by the old regime in the early days of Perestroika and Glasnost. There was an attempted coup against Gorbachev in 1991, and everybody thought the old communists were going to take over again. Rostropovich was in Paris at the time and he told his wife he was going down the street for cigarettes, because he knew she wouldn't have accepted what he really wanted to do. He went to the airport, bluffed his way through, and flew to Moscow with his cello. He went straight to the White House, which was barricaded against tank attacks.

Boris Yeltsin was inside and Rostropovich managed to get into the building. Yeltsin later wrote that his arrival there played a crucial role in restoring calm. Of course everyone knew who he was. He was given an armed guard, and while the communists were attacking the White House, Rostropovich had a photograph taken of himself and his armed guard, who had fallen asleep on his shoulder. Rostropovich was holding his guard's Kalashnikov in his arms knowing that the room could be minutes away from being invaded.

He showed me that astonishing photograph. He settled down to play the cello all night and it has been suggested that armed soldiers outside, on hearing him, may have been dissuaded from shelling the White House – an incredible thing to reflect on.

CANTOS SAGRADOS

The title Sacred Songs *is slightly misleading, as the poems you use are concerned with political repression in Latin America. What is liberation theology to you?*

The poems are deliberately coupled with traditional religious texts to emphasize a deeper solidarity with the poor. It was my interest in liberation theology which made me combine the poems of the Mothers of the Plaza de Mayo in Argentina with the texts of the Latin Mass in *Búsqueda,* an earlier music-theatre work. In many ways, one might say liberation theology was a passing phase in the church, and perhaps some of these theologians allowed themselves to be too influenced by Marxism. However, right at the heart of the Gospel is a preferential option for the poor. Christ has directed us to show solidarity with the poor – it's part of our religious tradition. With this composition, I wanted to give the poor a voice by setting the poetry of the Mothers of the Disappeared from Argentina, in a struggle with poverty but also with power.

TURBULENCE

In your music, meditative moments are often contrasted with turbulence.

I'm attracted by opposites in music and I'm intrigued by violence and serenity existing in the same sound space. Composers like Arvo Pärt or John Tavener, whose music I like a lot, don't do that. I'm interested in exploring the sacred in terms of turbulence and conflict as much as in sounds of serenity.

You use Gregorian chant in 'Tremunt Videntes Angeli', a hymn from the fifth century.

That's right. I visit the chant a lot in my work and there is something paradigmatically good about chant in church music. Perhaps something of the essence of it still has power to weave in modern music for the church. There's an element of tension in some of my liturgical music and that may reflect the church's engagement with modernity.

Has there been an evolution in your world view over the years?

Politically, I feel I've lost a lot of my youthful certainties. I grew up in a working-class part of Scotland, where the main industry was coal mining. My grandfather was a miner. I dabbled in the Marxist left at one time, but that has gone. I have grown cautious about ideologies, especially secular ideologies that have tried to replace religions. Marxism is certainly one of them. I feel a deep resonance in the Judaeo-Christian view of the world and of humanity. I make no apologies of being heir to that; it makes me think that the world is a good place to live in.

BEATIFICATION MASS

You were asked to write the beatification Mass for Cardinal Newman. What was the driving force behind your work? What gave you most joy?

I wanted to make the Mass melodies simple enough for ordinary people, yet infuse the music with a sense of grandeur and devotion. I felt great joy when I heard the music being sung by thousands in Glasgow and Birmingham. My whole life is a preparation for writing music for God – I do it every week for the little Dominican church in Glasgow. I certainly talked with many friends during the process. I experimented with ideas with my choir. I had huge support from Scottish bishops, clergy, musicians and lay people who had to defend me from malicious criticism and subterfuge.

Which moment was most fulfilling when attending the Mass?

I was especially pleased that the Pope and Monsignor Marini insisted on plainsong being sung at the open air Masses. This is the original music of the people, and it is now making its rightful way back into the Church's liturgy, after decades of exile. I was also asked to write other music for the Mass at Westminster Cathedral – a setting of 'Tu Es Petrus' and a fanfare for after the Gospel reading. This was scored for choir, organ, brass and percussion and was very different from the congregational Mass. I was thrilled to be able to do this too.

Why is Catholicism so central to you? Could you live without it?

No, I'd miss the ongoing search. I don't want to be settled. To come to the atheistic conclusion that there is no God would settle me too much. That might be surprising to people who think that Christians are set in their ways, but I find that our religious faith is a constant provocation to discover more, not just about oneself but also about the human state. I find it absolutely amazing and perplexing that God has sought out humanity so He can interact with us. His love for humanity is apparent in the life and presence of His son Jesus. I find that just too overwhelming an idea to give up. Faith is a path, but a path without anchorage is fraught with danger. My accomplice and companion on this path is the Catholic Church.

4

Brian Pierce

A holy mistake

As a boy growing up in Texas, Brian Pierce loved horses and nature. He wanted to study forestry, but his life took an unexpected turn when he was awarded a student scholarship to Peru. To this day, he wonders how he could have been chosen to receive a study grant that he had not even applied for. He also wonders how the programme had failed to take account of the violent political situation in Peru, where he suddenly found himself immersed as a naive 17-year-old. A holy mistake? Brian Pierce ended up falling in love with Latin America and its peoples.

When he returned to the USA and started college, he came by chance across some Dominican nuns, was entranced by their contemplative life and became a Dominican himself. He wrote about Martin de Porres, the black saint of the Americas.

Pierce ministered to the poor of South America, just like the first Dominicans, who arrived in La Española (Haiti and the Dominican Republic today) and vehemently protested at the exploitation by the Spanish invaders. He feels linked to his forerunners in the struggle for justice and peace. This led him, along with other Dominicans, to a water-only fast for 28 days in Union Square, New York in September 2002, to protest against the wars in Afghanistan and Iraq. He was a striking presence, young and handsome, in his white habit.

He himself wonders about the unexpected turns in his life: from an exchange student in Peru to a contemplative living in a mountain hut in Honduras, and then on to an ashram in Oklahoma and the sangha of the Vietnamese monk Thich

Nhat Hanh. When I ask him, 'How did all this come about?' he answers, 'Consider it another holy mistake. All of the major experiences in my life happened without me consciously directing them.'

It must have been 'the God in whom we live and move and have our being'. This phrase by St Paul to the Athenians is dear to Brian Pierce, as are the teachings of Meister Eckhart. Like Shigeto Oshida, he finds himself in the tradition of contemplative Dominicans who walk the path together with other spiritual pilgrims.

> Brian Pierce was born in 1960 in Kansas and raised in Texas. He is a friar of the Province of St Martin de Porres in the southern United States. He has lived and ministered in Peru, Honduras and Guatemala. He is presently assigned to Santa Sabina in Rome, accompanying the Order's contemplative cloistered nuns worldwide, of whom there are about 3,000 in 240 monasteries.

ASKING QUESTIONS IN PERU

What childhood memories do you cherish?

We were a very outdoor family. We grew up with horses and this taught me a lot about responsibility and enjoyment. The relationship with a horse is powerful because it is about fidelity and caring. It was an experience of bonding with nature. I had planned to study forestry, but after my stay in Peru, my life changed completely.

What happened?

As a high school foreign exchange student, I went to Cuzco. Peru was under a very brutal military dictatorship at that time. The day we arrived in Lima, the seven of us who were going to Cuczo, were told, 'The city is under a *toque de queda*, meaning that if you step outside of your house after 6 p.m., they'll shoot you dead.' We looked at each other in complete astonishment.

Three days later, I was in Cuzco. The military were everywhere. The family I stayed with lived right in front of the university, which was the focal point of all the tensions. The university students were rallying, and the army was suppressing the protests. As this happened before my eyes, I had no place to put this picture. I kept asking questions: 'Why are they killing each other? Why are the students throwing stones at the police? Why are the police shooting at the students?'

One day, something dreadful happened behind our house. There was gunfire all over the neighbourhood and everybody in the family got down on the floor. As we had glass doors on the second floor at the back of the house, we could see out onto the field behind the house. I saw a young university student running across, and behind him came a truck full of soldiers. I watched the soldiers beat and kill that young man, only 20 yards from our house. They beat him with guns, kicked his head in and shot him dead, then they picked up his body and threw it in the back of the truck. That day everything changed inside me; a wound came in me that I didn't know what to do with.

Were you the only one watching this student being killed?

No, the whole family was watching. After it happened I remember I turned to the family and asked why the soldiers had killed that boy. But no one said a word and I just held it inside of me for several years.

When I went back to the States, I finished high school and began to study forestry at the university, but I couldn't think about trees. I kept asking myself, 'What's wrong with the world?' So I switched my studies to Spanish and political science, hoping that it would help me to understand what had happened in Peru.

Did you find answers?

I did, eventually. I entered the Dominican Order after college graduation. Part of our training is to do some kind of ministry, so I contacted a woman called Eileen, who worked with refugees from the terrible wars in El Salvador, Nicaragua and Guatemala in the 1980s. Because I knew Spanish, I started working with Eileen. We would usually take two or three Salvadoran refugees to speak at a parish to inform people about what was happening in Central America. One day we took a young man named Juan, who had been studying to be a doctor in El Salvador. I stood next to him as a translator as he started telling his story. One day he was standing at a bus stop in San Salvador when a truck of soldiers came by and began to shoot everybody standing at the bus stop – they were all students. Then the soldiers picked up the bodies and threw them on the truck. Juan himself was wounded, but since they thought he was dead, they threw him onto the pile of dead bodies.

When he spoke of the bodies being thrown into the back of the truck, I couldn't continue translating. I started weeping uncontrollably, with this crowd of people in front of me. Something had broken inside me and it took me a couple of days to realize that it was because I had seen the same thing in Peru seven years earlier. For the first time I understood what I had witnessed.

What made you understand?

Juan said, 'I was a medical student, going to school, standing at a bus stop. Just because of that I was an enemy of the state because at the university, people were asking questions and calling for human rights.' Since I have lived in Central America I know this is true. There are questions you can't ask out loud without risking your life, like why peasants never acquire the land they work on.

JUST A DAY TRIP

Why did you become a Dominican?

Another holy mistake! I had started going to church at the college chapel every Sunday, enjoying it because it was the first time I was in a Mass with people who seemed happy; playing guitars and singing, with laughter and good preaching. One day, there was a note on the door of the church announcing a day trip to visit a monastery. I thought we were going to an archaeological site. It never occurred to me that we would see real people.

But the monastery turned out to be a very modern one. We were invited to Mass, where about 30 contemplative Dominican nuns were singing. After Mass they met with us in a big parlour, all of them wearing their habits; something I had never seen before. I remember one of the students asking the sisters, 'What do you do here?' and they answered, 'We pray.' The student insisted, 'But when you finish saying your prayers, then what do you do?' and they patiently answered, 'We keep on praying.' I thought to myself, 'This is the craziest thing I have ever heard!'

Afterwards, we had lunch and we laughed a lot. But two weeks later I borrowed somebody's car and drove back to that place, because I wanted to check if what they had said really was true. So I sneaked into the chapel and there they were, still praying, still singing!

What were you attracted by?

There was something palpable about the silence in that chapel that took hold of me and never let go. To this day I can taste that silence. After a couple of years I finally asked myself, 'Why do I keep going back?' I was not asking a vocation question at first. But the nuns were watching me. One of them would say a word to me, and another would leave a sandwich out on the table so that I could stay a little longer. After about two years I started doing some work for them, helping in their garden, and we became friends.

How did your parents react?

I didn't tell them until about six months before I entered the Order! They were as surprised as I was and I was as shocked as they were. My father is a Protestant and I only found out later what his side of the family really thought about Catholics. I lived in Texas and the noviciate was in South Carolina, on the Atlantic coast. So I set off. I had been told to bring three pairs of pants and a breviary; that was it. My mother cried when I left. I knew almost nothing about the Dominican Order, except that there were nuns who prayed all the time. I didn't even know who St Dominic was. And a Catholic Order dedicated to preaching seemed strange for someone from the Bible Belt of the southern United States.

How did you manage?

The first year was very hard for me. The novice master and I didn't click at all. He must have thought, 'How did this guy get

in? He doesn't even know why he is here!' I'm surprised they
didn't kick me out; but they didn't. Then one day I was given the
habit and I officially became a novice. It became clear to me that
the nuns had been like mothers to me. They had walked quietly
with me to this moment, without ever pushing me.

What did you study?

The big movement in theology at that time was liberation
theology. We studied Gustavo Gutierrez, John Sobrino, Leonardo
Boff. This theology came to me like fresh water because it
allowed me to see God's love for the poor. I understood that
one of the basics of liberation theology is the exodus story, God
leading the people from slavery to freedom. It gave me words
to understand my experience. I was able to go back to Peru to
study theology for a year.

TORTILLAS FOR PADRE BRIAN

*You also got involved with contemplation. Isn't it a huge leap
from liberation theology to Zen?*

Well, one day my Provincial said to me, 'The Order would like
to start a new community in Honduras. Would you like to go?'
I was packed before he finished his sentence! I wanted to go
back to that America that I had fallen in love with and that had
changed my life at 17. So I was sent to Honduras; I was ready to
save Latin America! I was on fire with everything, full of energy.
In the end, though, I reached a kind of burnout after six years
in Honduras.

What happened?

I went through a dark period. I loved Honduras and my work
there, but I reached the point where it all seemed futile. One day
I sat down with the brothers of my community and said, 'I can't
breathe here any more, I have to rediscover the contemplative
silence I once knew.' Once, while I had been working in the
villages in the mountains, a family had offered me a little hut as
a kind of retreat. There was no electricity, no water; just a river
nearby. I told my community I wanted to live there for a year,

which was a pretty radical proposal. We finally agreed that for a year I would spend three weeks of each month in that hut, and for one week a month I would come down and be with the brothers.

As the people in the villages had never had a priest living near them, some said, 'The villagers are so hungry for pastoral care that they won't give you one minute of peace!' What amazed me so deeply was that the people understood completely that I was there for silence. They never bothered me. I would visit one of the villages each Sunday for mass. About every three or four days they would send one of their children to my hut: 'Go and take Padre Brian some tortillas and don't make any noise!'

What did you find out about yourself?

I found my soul again. I found my centre again. At the end of the year, my Provincial from the States came down. We, as Dominicans, normally live in community, so he wanted to find out what in the world was going on! To my amazement, he offered me a chance to practise contemplation full time, but in the United States. I was happy and sad at the same time: sad because I had to leave Honduras, but happy because it led me to live in the Forest of Peace, a Benedictine monastic ashram in Oklahoma, for a year and a half.

How did you become interested in Meister Eckhart?

I simply had to find out how a Dominican could live a contemplative life. I knew that the German medieval theologian Eckhart was a mystic and a Dominican, so I set off on a journey to get to know him, suggesting to the nuns at the ashram that we study Eckhart together. For a year we read three volumes of his sermons together. It was wonderful! He gave me the words that I needed in order to go more deeply into my contemplative life as a Dominican. We then followed with six months study of Catherine of Siena. I had found what my heart was yearning for.

OSHIDA

Another Dominican, Shigeto Oshida founded a contemplative community north-west of Tokyo. Did you meet?

Unfortunately, I never met him. But Jim Campbell, one of the Dominicans I lived with in Honduras, told me a great story about him. Jim had been a fighter pilot in the US Air Force during the Second World War – a navigator on the bombers that bombed Japan. At the end of the War, he became a Dominican. When I met him, he was eaten up by remorse because of this episode in his life.

Jim had met Father Oshida once at a conference in the States, and he decided to go on a pilgrimage to ask forgiveness for having bombed Japan. When he finally found him in Takamori, he said, 'Father Oshida, I bombed your people during the War and I have come to ask for forgiveness.' Father Oshida looked at him and shouted, 'And I was in the Japanese anti-aircraft force in those days. I tried to shoot you down and I am sorry I missed!' They both laughed and embraced each other!

The way in which Father Oshida, this holy man, had showed Jim that they had both been part of the same evil, was very liberating for Jim. 'I am sorry I missed!' was the cry that set Jim free after 40 years of carrying this pain from the war. It was through Jim's stories that I came to revere Father Oshida.

It is a story typical of Father Oshida. I recognize his refreshing and authentic way of communicating, which I experienced when I interviewed him a few years before his death. You told me that Jim learned to meditate in silence in Takamori and that he taught you. What did the silence bring you?

First it brought me inner calm, but it guided me to something else too. I started reading Bede Griffiths, Meister Eckhart and Thich Nhat Hanh. Later, I visited Thây, as Thich Nhat Hanh is called by his pupils in France. It was his teaching on mindfulness that created a bridge to Meister Eckhart for me. Both of these mystics speak of equanimity; the inner stability to do whatever we do rooted in God's presence. I had been working myself to death in Honduras, to the point that I couldn't reach the inner silence any more. And now I realized that even in the 'busy-ness' of work we are held in this great Ground of God.

The story of Jesus in the boat with the disciples during the storm (Mk 4.35–41) has helped me very much. One day when I was reading it, I was struck by the fact that Jesus was asleep in the boat. The story just exploded for me at that point. I thought, 'This is what it's all about. There are times that life is like being in a boat in the middle of a storm!' Jesus first cries out, 'Peace!' and then He says, 'You of little faith.' What He is saying is, 'Don't you see me sleeping in perfect peace in the depths of your being, even in the storm? Did you think I was not here any more?' Mindfulness is the consciousness that Jesus is always in the boat with us. Once I touched that sleeping Christ deep within me I knew it was true. It's an experience I can't forget.

ENOUGH FOR MARTIN'S BUS TICKET

You developed a special relationship with Latin America and its black Dominican saint, Martin de Porres. How do locals view him?

Let me tell you a story about my friend Doña Paulina. When I was in Peru in 1985 as a theology student, I lived in Lima in a small priory of friars right next to the house where Martin de Porres was born in the sixteenth century. Right across the street, there is a poor woman, Paulina, who has been selling newspapers on the street corner for more than 40 years. She has a great devotion to St Martin. Every morning before she starts her work, she goes to Martin's statue in the house where he was born to have a little conversation with him. Paulina and I became friends. We would chat each morning as I waited for the bus on my way to classes. While I was headed for quiet classrooms to study theology, she would work 14 hours in the hot sun, breathing traffic fumes, to earn a dollar or two a day.

I have returned to Peru many times over the years, and once, when I went to see her, she told me that her two sons were in prison because they had been involved in a revolutionary movement. One of the sons was in prison in Puno, two days' travel from Lima. Paulina would save up her pennies for months so that she could take the bus to Puno a few times a year. She had been doing this for several years and was getting exhausted. One day when I was visiting again, I asked her about her son. She said, 'You don't know? I had a conversation with Martin the other day. I said, "Martin, I am too old and too sick to visit my son." So, I pulled out the money that a bus ticket costs and I set it next to the statue and said, "Martin, I have saved up enough to pay for your bus ticket, this will get you there and back; I want you to go and bring my son to Lima."' And in two weeks her son was transferred to Lima. She didn't ask for him to be set free; she just asked that he might be brought closer to her. Paulina is an amazing woman. Martin de Porres is her best friend: she tells him everything and asks his advice. I have frequently thought to myself, 'What I would give to have this kind of faith...!'

FAMILY MATTERS

You mentioned that your decision to become a Dominican caused some tension in your family. How serious was it?

My mother is a Catholic and my father is a Protestant. It was just a reality, I never thought about it growing up. Only later did I find out that my mother had never been allowed to visit my father's family while they were dating. My parents never told any of us. But when I entered the Dominican Order, things exploded. On my father's side of the family there was some real opposition. But my father made it very clear to his family that he supported his son totally. The only time that I ever saw my father cry was when he spoke to me one day about the pain this had caused him.

About six years ago my parents celebrated their fiftieth wedding anniversary; it was a wonderful experience. It was also the first time I had ever stepped back to contemplate the love between my parents, marvelling at the fact that they are still in love. I am aware that my basic experience of the faithful love of God comes from them.

I am quite sure that my interest in the world of interreligious dialogue is somehow linked to having been born in a family where ecumenism was a part of life. We never had an argument about religion in our family. I saw how my parents navigated the issue with such love for one another in the midst of the conflict that was going on in the background, with the wider family. That helped me when I became acquainted with India and Asia – Buddhism and Hinduism. I already had the tools for interreligious dialogue: respect, patience and love.

What connection do you see between East and West?

The East invites us to be conscious of our oneness with God. Most of us experience being separated from God, but in truth we can never be separate from God. It's the consciousness of 'I am' that the East emphasizes, while the West helps us to be conscious of the fact that 'we are'. When the first Dominican friars went to La Española, they were appalled by how the Spaniards treated the indigenous people. In the famous sermon of 1511 they asked, 'Are these not human beings? Are you so blind that you do not see the other person?' And they confronted the political powers whose greed had blinded them. It took courage for those friars to stand up and ask those questions. But they did so because Christianity is about the awareness that we walk the path together: we can't leave the little ones behind; we are all one body.

5
Maria Hanna

Killing Christians

'Leave Iraq to escape the violence? Where can we go? We are Christian Iraqis; this is our country! We were here before Islam. We have built schools, orphanages and hospitals for our people. Fanatical Muslims are now murdering Christians. The worst is that nothing is being reported by many media sources!'

Sister Maria Hanna, Prioress General of the Iraqi Dominican sisters, tells me about the countless church bombings, kidnappings and executions of Christians. Her mother house in Mosul is in ruins; the community dispersed. In a few days, she will return to her native Iraq as a kind of wandering prioress. 'I don't have a place to stay when I go back. I move each week to a different community; my sisters are scattered and afraid. When will the next attack come?'

She recalls the deaths of the Chaldean Catholic Archbishop Rahho of Mosul and the young Chaldean priest Ragheed, an alumnus of the Angelicum (the Dominican University of Thomas Aquinas in Rome), both brutally murdered as they were leaving church. A witness recollects how one of the killers screamed at Father Ragheed, reproaching him for not having closed down the church. The murderers pushed him to the ground and opened fire, killing him and his three subdeacons. In a letter written posthumously to Ragheed, a Muslim friend of his cried, 'In the name of what God of death have they killed you?'

Sister Maria has been deeply marked by the assassinations. On a rainy night in Rome, this courageous nun tells me her story. She tells of how she ran away from home when she was

only 12. How her grandfather gave his blessing for her to go to
the sisters because she wanted the Dominican Way to be hers.
After a life of service to her people – Christians and Muslims
alike – Sister Maria could finally retire to the contemplative
monastery of Chalais in France. Then war broke out in Iraq and
the retired prioress was recalled to her ruined country.

The following morning, when I go to the Angelicum, I notice
a portrait of a handsome young man in a black cassock whose
name is Ragheed Ganni, the murdered priest Sister Maria had
told me about. His stole had been given to Pope Benedict XVI by
the Chaldean bishops during their *ad limina* visit in 2009. The
Pope had received it with emotion.

> Sister Maria Hanna was born in 1930 in Qaraqosh on the
> Nineveh Plain in Iraq into a family of nine children. She
> is Prioress General of the Iraqi Dominican Sisters of St
> Catherine of Siena. The Dominican Order has been present
> in Iraq for several centuries and is consecrated in the Eastern
> Rite of the Catholic Church. The sisters engage in education,
> pastoral work and health care. In 1992, they opened the
> Al-Hayat maternity hospital. In 2009, Maria Hanna spoke
> at the Washington headquarters of the US Conference of
> Catholic Bishops about the gravity of the situation in Iraq.

Christians in Iraq

In 2003, Christians in Iraq were estimated at between 800,000
and 1.4 million. Most are Chaldeans, one of the oldest and
largest Christian populations in Iraq. They are Catholics who
are independent from Rome but recognize the Pope's authority.
As Christians have been the target of kidnappings and violent
attacks since the 2003 US-led invasion, roughly half the number
of Christians have fled the country. By 2010, the population was
estimated at about 400,000.

RUNNING AWAY TO BECOME A NUN

What are your most beautiful childhood memories?

We were a big Christian family. We lived together with my father's brothers and their families – there were about 20 of us under one roof! We cherished our friendships. What I particularly liked were the evenings when my father read from the New Testament and everybody in our neighbourhood came to listen. It is a beautiful memory that stays with me.

Why did you run away from home?

It was very difficult for me to leave my parents because I was the only girl in a family of nine children. But I was attracted to the life of the Dominican sisters who ran a small primary school, and I entered the convent because I wanted to pursue my studies. I now realize that it was extraordinary for such a young girl to run away from her parents to become a nun, but my grandfather gave me his blessing and promised to talk to my parents.

Why did you want to become a nun?

I was impressed by the kind and loving way in which the Dominican sisters ran our school. These nuns had actually built schools for girls because the state provided education only for boys. I wanted to be a contemplative nun from the age of 15 or 16, but this branch didn't exist in Iraq. My prioress at the time told me it was impossible for me to become a contemplative because the congregation needed me to work in our secondary schools.

So you became a teacher instead of a contemplative?

Yes. I taught at the St Thomas Aquinas Lyceum in Baghdad for eight years and then went to Algeria for four years, where I worked closely with the White Fathers. I taught science and biology in Arabic because the arabization of schools had started by then.

When I returned to Baghdad, I found that all schools had been nationalized after Saddam came to power in 1973. After teaching for another four years in Baghdad, I asked to be transferred to my home town Qaraqosh, because there was a great need for catechism. I often worked 45 hours a week, but I loved it because the pupils expressed their profound need and gratitude. During the first year of catechism we welcomed 1,000 summer students. In the second and third year the number rose to 3,500!

What about your dream to live as a contemplative nun?

At the end of my mandate as Prioress of our mother house in Mosul, I was able to retire and to go to the Dominican contemplative monastery of Chalais in France. It was an unforgettable experience!

But after 15 months in France, things became difficult in Iraq. Sanctions had been applied, and when American troops invaded I could no longer continue my quiet retreat. So, I went back. At our general Chapter one year after the invasion, I was elected Prioress General.

TOTALLY DESPERATE

What are the circumstances you have to live in today?

We are totally desperate. Moreover, we are Christians – a minority in Iraq. We have always been willing to help everybody, but now we feel deserted. Our minority position is taken advantage of by various political parties. Everyone who is not Muslim has been warned to leave the country. A lot of people have received letters with a bullet inside. It is very difficult to describe the situation because it is so complex. Politics, culture and religion are intertwined. Moreover, we don't know who is fighting whom.

How are Christians perceived by the local people?

The Christian minority has always been appreciated because it has played an active role in developing the cultural, economic and scientific life of the country. **But we are all** in the same situation now and everyone in the neighbourhood has become very close to each other.

What were your most difficult moments?

The assassinations of Archbishop Rahho of Mosul and young Father Ragheed were more than we could take.

Abouna [Father] Ragheed had just finished his studies at the Angelicum. He was about to return to Rome to do his PhD when he was killed along with three subdeacons in June 2007, as they were leaving the Church of the Holy Spirit in Mosul where they had celebrated Mass. Especially moving was the testimony of the wife of one of the subdeacons, who is now living as an exile in Syria. She spoke out on the first anniversary of the deaths: 'At a certain point, the car was stopped by armed men. Father Ragheed could have fled, but he did not want to because he knew they were looking for him. They forced us to get out of the car and led me away. Then one of the killers screamed at Father Ragheed, "I told you to close down the church. Why didn't you do so? Why are you still here?" He simply answered, "How can I close down the house of God?" They pushed him to the ground, and he had only enough time to gesture to me with his head that I should run away. Then they opened fire and killed all four of them.'

IN DEATH, GIVING BECOMES INFINITE

What happened to the Archbishop?

In February 2008, less than a year after the Archbishop had celebrated the burial of Father Ragheed, he too was seized by gunmen, in the Al-Nur district of Mosul. Three people who were with Father Rahho were killed and he was kidnapped. There was blood on the ground, but we didn't know if he was wounded or not. There was no news about him for days and then we heard he had been killed and left in a shallow grave close to the city. Searching for his body was a very painful experience. When we found him, we buried him in a Christian village. The grief and sadness was unbearable. Bishop Rahho was greatly loved; he had opened orphanages and taken special care of handicapped children.

In his will, Archbishop Rahho called upon the Iraqi Christian community to work with Muslim and Yazidi Iraqis to develop

ties across religious divides. Some excerpts were published:
'Death is a dreadful reality, more dreadful than any other, and
each one of us must deal with it. People who give their lives
express the profound faith they have in God and their trust in
Him. Death means a stop to this giving to God and others in
order to open up and give oneself again, without end or flaw.
Life means fully placing oneself in the hands of God. In death,
giving becomes infinite in eternal life. I call all of you to be open
to our Muslim and Yazidi brothers.'

What were the reactions to these assassinations?

These kidnappings and killings have underlined the precarious
conditions facing Christians in Iraq and have induced tens of
thousands of Christian families to leave their homes; in many
cases leaving Iraq entirely.

Can't you leave Iraq?

Impossible! This is our country, we are Christian Iraqi. We
are among the oldest inhabitants of this country. Although we
are attacked by Muslim fanatics, even Muslims ask us to stay
because they say they'd feel lost without us. People don't understand that a political game is being played between Iran, Saudi
Arabia and Syria. The situation is very complicated. Besides, we
can't abandon those who have been placed in our care: the poor,
the vulnerable, the widows and their children.

DON'T THEY GET TIRED OF KILLING?

Have the convent buildings been attacked?

At the mother house in Mosul and at the convent of Our Lady
of Al-Hadbaah in Mosul, there have been many explosions.
Once, a car bomb went off at the entrance of the mother house,
causing a fire which did considerable damage. Two months later,
there was another car bomb. One day, I was on the road to visit
a community when I got a phone call: our mother house near
Mosul had suffered yet another bomb attack. Three men had
jumped over the walls and put bombs right opposite the window
at the entrance. Another time, it was a rocket-propelled grenade.

Once, they set fire to a propane can and left it in front of our gate. Another time, a device was planted inside the fence next to the mother house and when it exploded all the windows were blown out and the wooden doors and iron gates destroyed.

Today our windows are covered with nylon instead of glass or with bricks to prevent explosive devices being thrown inside. Even the entrances to the house are covered with bricks for security. Our orphanage in Talkief has also suffered many bombings, as have our convents in other parts of Iraq.

How do you see the future?

At the moment, we see none. We sometimes hope normal life might resume, but we often hope in vain. We were happy when the government had finally decided on a piece of land for us so that we could transfer our mother house from Mosul to Qaraqosh. But when everybody seemed to have agreed, the permission was withdrawn.

Our convent in Mosul used to be the permanent residence of some 60 sisters: novices, students, older sisters and those who worked in Mosul. After the bombings, only four sisters stayed. In 2006, we had to leave the house because the situation had become too dangerous. The streets were littered with corpses. People were kidnapped before our eyes. It was very difficult; hygiene became problematic. In the end, we decided to leave in order to protect our older and sick sisters.

Do you revolt against God?

Yes, yes, yes, of course! I constantly cry, 'Where are You? Don't You see?' When another entire family is massacred again, I ask Him desperately why this can happen. The only answer is our faith, nothing else.

Don't you ever doubt?

Yes, there are times... for instance when there was an attack on a bus taking students from Qaraqosh to Mosul University. Two bombs went off. At the first blast, a man got out of his car to warn the students to stay inside the bus. Then the second bomb exploded and killed him. There were terrible scenes. Many of the students lost eyes, arms or legs or were terribly maimed. A

7-year-old boy who overheard adults talking about the attack said, 'Who are these people? Don't they get tired of killing?' One of our sisters who lives in Florence saw the images on the internet. She spent three days and nights without eating. All she could do was cry.

What do you think about dialogue with Islam?

It is really very difficult. Nevertheless, some of our sisters in the schools succeed in building good relationships with the students and their parents, most of whom are Muslim. The sisters are extraordinary; they welcome everybody with love and respect and try to pursue a dialogue.

ENTIRELY THEIR DECISION

Isn't Christianity looked down on?

Not in Iraq, no. A lot of Muslims are converting to Christianity at the moment because they see what is happening: all these attacks, the killings, the lies...

But converting to Christianity is even more dangerous.

Yes, they know. That's why they don't openly declare themselves to be Christian, although some do so in the north of Iraq. At least 7,000 Muslims have converted to Christianity. It's dangerous for them, though. If somebody's family knew, he would be killed. That's why neither priests nor friars ever proselytize or ask anyone to speak openly about their faith. The initiative to convert is entirely theirs. We don't do anything to encourage them – quite the opposite! But it seems that they are willing to take the risk because of faith. They see Jesus as their saviour, someone who rescues people from persecutors. This concept doesn't exist in Islam.

It is true that we are not allowed to preach, but Muslims have been ingenious in finding ways to make contact with our priests and brothers because they want to know more about Christianity. Many of them have become friends.

Is it still possible to pray in situations like these?

We take a lot of strength from being connected to the oriental traditions. We use Aramaic, the language Jesus spoke, for our prayers in our Christian communities in the village, while Arabic is the language of our monastic daily office. The words of the church fathers, and especially the psalms, are a great consolation because we read our own lives, all the pain and sorrow, in the psalms right now.

How are the sisters perceived by local people?

A year ago, one of our sisters was in hospital. A Muslim doctor and his team wanted to visit her. In the hallway, he addressed his students, 'Pay attention to what I have to tell you. You have to realize that I wouldn't be here if it weren't for this woman who is lying here ill in bed.' The students looked at him in surprise and he continued, 'I was able to become a doctor because I knew the sisters would always stand up for me. Once, when I wanted to leave school, these Dominicans came to my parents to urge me to continue my studies. So, these nuns deserve our respect, don't ever let them down!'

This kind of story is an encouragement, but sadly all our schools have been nationalized. The new generation of students doesn't know what we have accomplished. None of our sisters is teaching any more.

How do you look back on your life?

I can't for the moment. We are here in Iraq to stay. We nourish hope for the future and love for our people.

ALLOWED TO BE PROVOKED

What do you think about Islam coming to Europe?

It hurts me. Islam has hurt me a lot. Muslims and their mentality are not well known. We need time to get to know one another. There are a lot of good things. Don't misunderstand me: I have a lot of Muslim friends and I love them with all my heart, but they are different. I am afraid for Europe; it doesn't know what is coming.

What are you afraid of?

Violence. It is not Islam itself that is violent but those Muslims who allow themselves to be provoked by fanatics. Fanatic Islam is very much alive. I am worried about the diminishing presence of Christians. How long can we resist? We can't advise people not to leave the country. Everybody has to decide for themselves. I know some families who have left Iraq and who now live in extremely difficult conditions in the surrounding countries.

I'm also concerned about the 145 sisters who depend on me, 103 of whom live in Iraq. The others are working outside the country or are novices. Our work must go on, we have to prepare new sisters. It is a real comfort to know that there are people praying for us and supporting us, like the Dominican sisters in America.

Who is a source of inspiration to you?

Our own friars and sisters. I can give two examples. In Baghdad, the Dominican friars have set up an open university. The Korean Dominican painter Kim En Joong will colour the six-metre-high rose window. The goal is to create an environment of dialogue, study and encounter. We want Iraqis to come, meet and reconcile.

Another extraordinary thing happened last month. All but two hospitals in Baghdad had closed because of the violence. Our sisters seemed to be the only ones who had managed to keep them open! One was the hospital of Al-Hayat, which offers a 24-hour emergency clinic, and the other was kept open by our sisters of the Presentation of Tours. Every other hospital had closed but our sisters stayed when things were at their most difficult. People came from all over Iraq, not only from Baghdad. The sister students from the University of Babel even joined the convent to be able to help the sisters with their work.

What can I wish you for your return to Iraq?

Peace, nothing else. Don't wish me a good journey back to Iraq – all that is unimportant. When I was in America, I was asked, 'What is peace?' I answered, 'Peace is to live as you do, not differently.'

6

Henri Burin des Roziers

Against the grain

'The south of Pará is the land of blood and death, corruption and shame. Law is set by guns.' This is how Frei Henri Burin des Roziers describes the Amazonian villages where he has been working for more than 30 years as a lawyer defending the *sem terra* – the landless peasants who claim the right to cultivate and live on land promised to them by the Brazilian constitution. Who can understand why this bright lawyer, educated at the best institutions in Europe, raised in the French aristocracy, renounced worldly luxuries to spend his life among landless peasants?

In 2000, for the first time in the history of Brazil, Burin des Roziers succeeded in having a *fazendeiro*, a big landowner, condemned in court for having ordered the assassination of a union leader. As a result, Henri's name was put on a death list. An idle threat? Certainly not! In 2005, the world was shocked by the brutal murder of his colleague, the 73-year-old American missionary, Dorothy Stang, who had also tirelessly defended the peasants against the *fazendeiros*. Her murder sent a shiver through the country and the international community. Henri has been given police protection whenever he is travelling in the state of Pará, where violence has become common and casual. Being a *pistoleiro* there is a job like any other.

In the Paris apartment of his brother Michel, where he is staying temporarily for health reasons, Henri recalls some of his lawsuits. But he is no pessimistic struggler. On the contrary, the Paris flat rings with laughter at his jokes. At the end of the interview, he entrusts to me his dream. Although his health is not good, he is eager to return to Brazil. 'The Indians are my people,' he says. 'I can see something of God where I live; I am a lucky man!'

Henri Burin des Roziers was born in 1930 in Paris, to an upper-middle-class family. He studied law at the Sorbonne and at Cambridge University, where he met the Dominican Yves Congar. Following his ordination as a Dominican preacher, he became almoner to the students in law and economics in Paris during the events of 1968, and then worked in the associations defending the rights of immigrant workers. In 1978 he travelled to Brazil, where he works as a lawyer on behalf of the landless peasants of the Amazon forest. In June 2000, he secured the first conviction of a *fazendeiro*, responsible for the murder of a union leader. He is a Knight of the French Legion of Honour for his work for human rights, and was awarded the Ludovic Trarieux international human rights prize.

FAR WEST

You are working in Pará, one of the most violent states of Brazil. What is the atmosphere like in the towns where you live?

I live in Xinguara, a small town of 40,000 inhabitants in southern Pará. The region is in full expansion. Its greatest wealth is its livestock farming, with millions of head of cattle. Conflicts over land are extremely violent. The towns are growing fast; their outskirts drawing the poor and unemployed. Drug use is consequently widespread. Pará is ruled over by very large landowners – *fazendeiros*. In my municipality, for instance, one family enterprise owns more than 80,000 hectares, holding 250,000 head of livestock. One very large farm with links to a bank recently acquired, over a period of three years, 400,000 hectares with 500,000 cattle.

You are a lawyer for the Pastoral Land Commission. We don't have this kind of pastoral work in the West. What is it about?

The Church set up this Commission in the 1970s, to defend the rights of peasants violently expelled from their lands, and of farm workers treated like slaves. The Catholic Church's action in favour of the rural poor finds its roots in Vatican II and liberation theology. I have been working as a lawyer for the Land Commission for 30 years.

And you have been threatened for practising in that capacity. But why is land such a problem in Brazil?

Since the conquest and colonisation by Portugal in the sixteenth century, the concentration of land ownership has been huge, as has inequality.

In Brazil, the land belongs to the State, which can sell it to private individuals, who then have property deeds. But much land has not been sold, and according to the constitution, it should be used for agrarian reform – in other words, given to the landless peasants. But the *fazendeiros* always maintain that the land belongs to them, using dubious deeds and other false arguments to support their claims. It is estimated that 50 per cent of land in Pará has been acquired in this way.

The trials to punish these abuses drag on in the courts for years. The landowners – moneyed and enjoying social, economic and political influence – use all the means at their disposal – including corruption, threats and murder – and almost always win these cases. For their part, in order to pressurize the authorities and to be able to survive, the peasants occupy small parcels of a few hectares on the immense farms that they know are illegal. The *fazendeiros*, with their *pistoleiros* and their private militias, drive them off the land, without awaiting the judge's decision. That's the story of the land disputes.

Are these fazendeiros authorized to use force?

Very often, yes. Just before I left for France, on Christmas Day, there was a tragedy in a community where 80 families were occupying a piece of land. The *fazendeiro* wanted to evict them. The judge had had the eviction order suspended, but the town's military commander nevertheless arrived with eight masked and heavily armed men. Picture the scene: with their faces masked, they opened fire on the car of the leader of these families, who was leaving, and then they drove everybody off. This is how the landowners evict people by force even before the end of a trial.

What role is played by the legal and political systems?

More than 100 members of parliament have large agricultural holdings, and they fight to pass laws in their favour, so that they can grow at the expense of the peasants. Even today, you see, the *fazendeiro* lobby is extremely important.

Impunity is a huge problem in Brazil. During the 30 years I have been working in Pará, some 1,500 peasants, union activists, lawyers, priests and nuns have been murdered in land disputes. Only 92 cases have been brought to trial, and only eight instigators have been found guilty – and only one of them is actually in prison. That is the person who ordered the murder of Sister Dorothy Stang. Only one! So you see: violence and impunity rule. They are almost absolute!

WANTED

You were the first to secure the conviction of a fazendeiro. That caused ructions. What is the state of play?

In the late 1980s and early 90s, the *fazendeiros* in my region decided to eliminate the rural labourers' union of the Rio Maria municipality because it supported land occupation. They hired hitmen, and their first target was the chairman of the union. Next they drew up a list of union members and church people to assassinate. In December 1991, they murdered the second union chairman, a very well-known man, Expedito Ribeiro de Souza. Two months previously, *Le Monde Diplomatique* had dedicated a whole page to him, under the headline, 'This man is marked for assassination!' The outcry at his murder mobilized public opinion to insist that justice be done.

And you accepted to be the lawyer.

Yes. When an investigation starts, the lawyers must get to the scene immediately, before all the evidence disappears. I had already bought a ticket to leave for Central America when Expedito was killed. I offered my services because there wasn't another lawyer nearby. This murder had been ordered by a very powerful *fazendeiro* who enjoyed considerable support from lobbies, including in parliament. In the end, we succeeded in getting him condemned, but with great difficulty.

As a result, the large landowners have put a price on your head. Aren't you afraid?

The first threats directed at me came around 1985. Naturally, I was not unmoved to see my name on a wanted list published in the papers! But it has become common. Many people are assassinated by the *pistoleiros*. In Brazil, killing people has become a job like any other. In 1995, I received a letter from brother Timothy Radcliffe, head of the Dominican Order, saying, 'These *fazendeiros* won't hesitate to use any lie to discredit someone! But don't lose faith; your brothers all over the world are with you. We are very proud of everything you do for the rights of the peasants.' I really appreciated that support. It is true that you can find the pay scales of hitmen in the papers. A union official is more expensive than a mere worker, a bishop more expensive than a curate. At the time, the price on my head was around £30,000. But recently, rumour has it that the prices have changed. Apparently I am now worth no more than £20,000! I've been devalued! (*Laughs*)

How can you live under permanent threat?

First, there is a lot of violence in our region, be it for robbery, drugs, vengeance or political reasons. Violence is part of life. Currently, people barricade themselves in their homes and don't go out at night. Sometimes, the home help will arrive at our place in the morning and tell us that in her rather isolated district three or four people were murdered during the night. I'm not afraid. But if I had a wife and children, I would not take the same risks.

It seems that slave labour still exists in Brazil.

There are an estimated 25,000 farm workers in Brazil who are subjected to slave labour. The estates are immense and need a large workforce. Many landowners are out for maximum profit at minimum cost. So they recruit hundreds of workers from the poorest and remotest regions where there is no work, and promise them generous salaries. Then they take them to their *fazendas,* far from any town, so the workers can't leave. Once there, they receive much less money than promised. What's more, workers are obliged to buy provisions on credit at the farm store, where prices are much higher than in the distant town. In this way, they have to spend more than they earn, and end up in debt.

If they try to leave, they will sometimes have to cover over 50 kilometres on foot in the forests, where they might meet armed guards. So they work on these farms like slaves. They have lost their freedom.

TRAGIC CASES

You were the subject of a smear campaign for having denounced police torture.

As a lawyer for the Pastoral Land Commission, I usually take on only land cases, of which there are already many. But every so often there are truly tragic cases that no lawyer wants to take on.

One day in 2001, a woman told me, 'My 15-year-old son was taken by the police. He was tortured for three days, and now he is mad.' You should know, in Brazil, torture is common in police stations. This mother begged me to take on the case, saying, 'Brother Henri, they have destroyed my son, my family. I would like this trial, at least, to prevent any other mother from suffering the same thing.'

So I accepted, on certain conditions. I told her, 'The legal work alone will not be enough to get these torturers sentenced. This trial will only work if there is political pressure. If you accept to give interviews to the television, radio and press, to denounce what they did to your son, then the outrage of public opinion can move the trial forward and win a guilty verdict. You will be taking a huge risk, because all the police in the state will do their utmost to keep their colleagues from being condemned.' She accepted.

She suffered a great deal, and had to leave the region, such were the persecution and threats. In addition, a smear campaign was launched against myself and the judge, who also received threats.

The case was so shocking that in 2001 Amnesty International chose it as one of the ten emblematic torture cases for that year. In the end, the policemen were given prison sentences and dismissed from the police force. But still today, one of them – sentenced to eight years in prison – remains at large, thanks to the complicity of the police and the courts. So we continue to push for his prison sentence to be executed. But at least the police no longer torture people in Xinguara and the surrounding region. The victim is still receiving medical treatment in the capital, at the state's expense.

What makes you fight so obstinately for justice?

Look at the landless peasants! They are just as stubborn. When you witness the illegal eviction of families who have lost everything, it grips you. When I visit a camp of landless folk in Brazil and I see the disease, hunger and threats; the families camped on a strip of land 15 metres wide between the road and the barbed-wire fence of a *fazenda* that extends for thousands of hectares – often uncultivated – which should be allocated to them but from which they have been violently evicted on the grounds of a title deed that is probably false, it is impossible not to react. And the freedom given me by my religious vocation in the Dominican Order! That freedom, at least, must be good for something.

BEATITUDES

You must have asked yourself many questions about God. Who is He? Why these murders? Have you found any answers?

I have found an answer, which might seem commonplace to you, but is no longer for me. In the past, the Bible hardly interested me, because I didn't see much connection with my own life, even while studying theology. When, after 1968, I came into contact with the foreign workers in the working-class districts of France and felt the full impact of discrimination and injustice, that was when I rediscovered the Gospel. But it was in Brazil, with the Pastoral Land Commission and liberation theology, reading the Bible from the perspective of the poor, their suffering and struggle, that I discovered the relevance of the Bible to life.

When I am among my people, the landless, that's when I feel that I am living and seeing live around me the blessings of the Gospel:

> Blessed are the poor in spirit, for the Kingdom of Heaven belongs to them. Blessed are those who mourn, for they shall be comforted. Blessed are those who hunger and thirst for righteousness, for they shall be satisfied. Blessed are those who are persecuted for righteousness's sake, for the Kingdom of Heaven belongs to them. Blessed are you when others revile you and persecute you and utter all kinds of evil against you falsely on my account, for your reward is great in Heaven. (*Mt. 5.1–12*)

When I am in Brazil, I witness so much of the Gospel. I see solidarity in extreme poverty, the sharing and thus the multiplying of bread, the thirst for justice, people who are scorned and persecuted, fighting for their human dignity as sons of God. When I'm there, I feel confident and in alignment with the Gospel and my Dominican vocation. I miss having a family of my own, but at the same time that renunciation has been an enormous resource, because it allows me to dedicate myself to this cause.

I tell you humbly that I believe in prayer, contemplation and Mass, but there, with them, I feel very close to Jesus, who is the Poor Man, chiefly present among the poor. Now I understand the meaning of the words 'God is Love'. They are no longer just words for me, because somehow I see a little of the face of that God where I am living.

BOURGEOISIE

You renounced the advantages of your family and chose a different direction in life. What were your reasons?

But I have renounced nothing! I am much happier where I live now in Brazil than I was in Paris. It's my personality, my vocation. St Dominic was so radical, so driven by the material and spiritual distress of the poor, that I believe I am following that line of Dominican history. In reality, I am very lucky, and happy! I have the chance to live the Gospel in actual solidarity with the excluded of the Earth. The material wealth I have given up never interested me. By contrast, the fight for justice has always deeply motivated me.

Even as a child?

Yes. I always suffered a little from living in a rich family, because of the inequality I saw. I was strongly marked by my experiences as a student. Just after the War, I was part of a St Vincent de Paul Society group that went into the working-class districts. I saw many families in very small, overcrowded accommodation, with problems of health and promiscuity. It at once spoke to me and motivated me. I often wondered why I lived in such a comfortable environment and they did not.

How did your parents react when you announced your decision to work as a labourer?

My parents were concerned, but they respected my wishes. I worked on public transport, in public works projects, with immigrants. Before I entered the Dominican Order, they simply asked me to finish my law thesis. I had not yet been to Cambridge then. The troubles of May 1968 weren't easy for them. But I have no regrets about those days. The movement of May '68 represented the dream of a different society: fair, brotherly, inclusive. It is important to dream!

Later, when I left for Brazil, my parents respected my decision. They have always supported me in my vocation and my work. I am grateful to my family for having allowed me to live those things.

Were you happy as a child?

Yes and no, because my childhood coincided with the Second World War. I was ten when war broke out. My father was a prisoner for a year and a half, and three of his brothers were in the Free French Forces of General de Gaulle. Others were deported. That episode marked me considerably.

At 15, I experienced the Allied landing, and later the victory – that was absolutely fantastic. I remember well the moment when my uncles who had been deported or were in the Allied forces, reappeared. My grandmother's joy was immense.

One of your uncles was one of de Gaulle's companions.

Yes, my uncle Étienne Burin des Roziers joined de Gaulle in London in 1942. After the War, he was ambassador to Warsaw, and then Secretary General to the Presidency of the Republic under de Gaulle.

I remember the evening, during the War, when we were discreetly listening to General de Gaulle's calls on *France Libre* radio. We were still afraid for those who had been deported.

During the war, I felt the same thirst for independence among the French people that I found later during other wars of independence in Tunisia, Algeria and Morocco. Today, I see the same courage in the movements of the landless peasants who are massacred, slandered, imprisoned. This hunger for dignity of a whole population is impressive.

DOMINICAN

Why did you choose the Dominicans?

At the end of my compulsory military service, that I served in North Africa, as did all in those generations, I was thinking of a religious life. I had obtained a grant to go to England to write a thesis on comparative law, and that was where I met Father Yves Congar, who had been exiled by Pope Pius XII following the restriction of the worker priests. He was living in the small Blackfriars community in Cambridge. I saw him suffering in his exile, banned from publishing or attending conferences, but retaining an impressive inner freedom and continuing to work along lines that interested me and questioned many things, such as the functioning of the Church at the time. He was rehabilitated a few years later and was one of the great experts on Vatican II. His solidarity with the worker-priests and the working class from which the Church had cut itself off, also opened me up to the Dominicans' work for the poor. It was at the end of my year at Cambridge University that I decided to become a Dominican.

What was it that touched you in Yves Congar?

I felt his great freedom in relation to the Vatican, while all the while obeying the prohibition imposed upon him. I noticed that he had the full support of the community in his province in France, which considered his punishment unjust and scandalous.

I thought about that a lot. The Dominican Order has its priorities and preferences, but it does not impose. Many fellow brothers of my generation left the large convents, with the agreement of their superiors, to form small communities in suburban districts; not in order to preach, but to discover the new culture germinating in working-class areas and to work alongside the workers. Having been in contact with Dominicans exiled by dictatorships, victims of torture, I had the dream of going to Latin America. The Dominicans accepted and supported me. I kept in touch with Congar. Whenever I came to Europe, I would always go to see him, until his death in 1995.

A TRUE MYSTIC

Who inspired you during that time?

In 1990, I spent a sabbatical year in Central America, including four months in Guatemala, in the region where Bartolomé de Las Casas had been. While there, I spent much of my time observing the Indians in the mountains and meditating on Bartolomé.

His impassioned defence of the Indian slaves of the Spanish colonists, their right to freedom and dignity, to respect for their land and culture, that ran so much against the grain of the mentality at that time – of both society and Church – left a deep impression on me. In the sixteenth century, the Indians weren't regarded as human. You doubtless know the famous words of Dominican Antonio de Montesinos, in a sermon to *fazendeiros* in 1511: 'Are they (*the Indians*) not human beings?' These words are just as powerful today, in land disputes. In another way, the same problem persists in the exploitation of farm labourers and landless peasants by the landowners, today's *conquistadores*. The Pastoral Land Commission is a cry against the power of oppression and injustice.

If I have been impressed by a true mystic, it is Bartolomé de Las Casas. He was a great lawyer who placed his intellectual wealth at the service of the poorest. For me, he is the founder of human rights.

There are many evangelical churches in Brazil. What is their influence?

They are very important. In smaller towns of 30,000 to 40,000 inhabitants like mine, there are always 10 or 20 evangelical churches. Consequently, the Catholic church has been influenced to some extent by the evangelicals, who are growing in numbers. It borrows from them the emotional flavour: the gestures, the music, the testimonials of healing and conversion. It is true, though, that the evangelical churches do not share the Catholic Church's continued concern for social affairs.

You are a Knight of the Legion of Honour and have been awarded the Ludovic Trarieux international human rights prize. But you were not happy with these honours!

It is true, when I received my first honour, I told myself that I hadn't come to Brazil to receive prizes! But I was encouraged to give it more thought. Being awarded a prize of this kind can help in getting more media attention. So I accepted the Legion of Honour, so that we could use it as an excuse to stage an event that would serve the cause of agrarian reform. Rather exceptionally, I asked for the French Ambassador to Brazil to come and decorate me in our small town. This made it possible during the ceremony to mention the land disputes and murders with impunity. Since the Ambassador had come in an official capacity to give me the medal, the press could say, 'Brother Henri has the support of his country!' There was even a bottle of champagne, for an otherwise simple ceremony. This decoration provided considerable support to the victims of violence I was defending.

CRISIS OF CONSCIENCE

But you have experienced difficult times too.

I went through a serious crisis of conscience in 1988 and 1989. I was totally isolated, 2,500 kilometres away from the nearest official Dominican community, living alone with a parish priest. Because communal life is fundamental to the Dominicans, I felt that I was not being faithful to the precepts.

So I went to a priory to see a wise and very respected old Dominican, and I confided my state of mind to him. He listened to me, then took the acts of a general Chapter of the Dominicans that defined one of the Order's priorities as being at new frontiers, new challenges in the world, including the challenge of life and death. He said, 'Where you are, you are exactly faithful to our precepts. You are in Amazonia, confronting an extremely important challenge: the challenge of land, the life-and-death challenge of the landless peasants you are defending!' He added, 'Community doesn't just mean physical presence; it also exists in the communion of spiritual choice, even if the members of the community are not together. You are there because you are exactly realizing an option of our Province.' His words greatly relieved me. And indeed, the Dominican Province in Brazil has always supported me.

ETERNITY

During our correspondence, you quoted St Dominic: 'I shall be more useful to you after my death.' Do you really have such absolute faith?

I deeply believe that life does not stop; that life goes on mysteriously. Life in the Kingdom of God is a mystery. I deeply believe that those who leave us continue to live.

Do you expect to see them again?

I think so. I am convinced that the mystical presence and intercession of St Dominic is fundamental. He continues to inspire his brothers from where he is to be faithful to the mission of the

Order. I deeply believe that. I believe it is important to pray to our founder to accompany and help us. During Mass, I always keep silence when I reach the 'communion of the saints'. It is the moment to think of our dead who accompany us and who, perhaps, can be of more help to us. I am also convinced that Jesus Christ is present when we celebrate Mass, mysteriously revived to show us that life does not end here below.

Do you still have a dream?

I would like to be buried discreetly in land won through struggle by the peasants who have suffered so much, and with whom I have shown solidarity in my way so that they can live in greater dignity. And the children who pass by would say, 'Ah, that's Brother Henri – he lived here and fought with us!' That is my dream. I don't know if I'll be able to return to Brazil, given my current state of health. It is in God's hands!

7
Margaret Ormond

COLUMBUS, OHIO; INTERVIEW IN ROME

A loving glance

Margaret Ormond grew up in an Irish-American Catholic family, with Jewish neighbours, in Brooklyn, New York. She quickly became aware that diversity was a natural thing. Her parents would send their Jewish neighbour a Hanukkah card and they would get a Christmas card back. As a child travelling on her own by train to school in Manhattan, she would pass the Russian Embassy and sense that the world was larger than her neighbourhood.

She was an outgoing and lively girl who liked dancing and going out with friends, and she surprised everybody, and most of all her parents, when she told them she wanted to be a Dominican sister. 'Not you!' they said. 'If one of the others had chosen a religious life, we wouldn't have been surprised.' So, why did young Margaret, back in the 1960s, go to a convent where she was not even allowed pocket money?

Her story is intriguing and has maintained an international dimension because she became one of the founders and the first Coordinator of Dominican Sisters International. This involved Margaret travelling all over the world to encourage Dominican sisters in desperate situations. She radiates with pride when she tells me of their courage. But she strikes me as being the right kind of leader: tender yet strong and drawing inspiration from the depths of her being, as well as from Gospel stories where Jesus is reaching out to downtrodden people.

On her travels, preaching and instructing others how to preach, Margaret Ormond has inspired and heartened many on the road. Yet, her most profound experience was being consoled herself when she was visiting a poor neighbourhood on the outskirts of San Salvador. There she found herself crying in the face of so much deprivation. Unexpectedly, her tears were wiped from her eyes by a little girl standing nearby.

Margaret Ormond was born in Brooklyn, New York, in 1943 and studied history in college in America, and theology in Rome. She spent most of her ministerial life in Connecticut, Ohio and Illinois, where she worked in education, formation and leadership. In 1998, she became the first Coordinator of Dominican Sisters International. She is currently the Prioress of a new community founded in 2009, the Dominican Sisters of Peace, which is present in 37 US states and 5 different countries.

EXPERIENCING MORE

Childhood memories can be very influential, even if we are not always conscious of them. Do you remember specific formative moments?

In high school, we had a Dominican sister for religion class. She encouraged us 'to be a saint because a saint is someone who believes that God loves her'. That captivated me, even though I was only a teenager. I wanted everybody to experience God's loving glance!

Another thing that formed me is that I became interested in history and in current events. On my way to school in Manhattan, I passed the Russian Embassy, which made me aware of being in a bigger world than just my own country. Other happenings, such as not having school during the Cuban missile crisis, broadened my perspective. I felt linked to a bigger world and enjoyed studying about past events.

So why did your main focus of interest become theology?

I was fascinated by God's love for me, and I wanted to know more about that. I have five siblings, but the singular experience that God loved me was very special. Many factors nurtured and confirmed that reality, like becoming involved in service projects and working with the elderly after school. I didn't question God, not in my early years; I was not a rebel. In later life, when I accompanied many people especially in the face of loss, it became different. In my college years, my cousin Billy was killed in a terrible accident. I was so angry at God and asked him why Billy was killed. But my aunt, Billy's mother, shared her own struggle with me: 'Margaret, I can either become bitter or better.' Her words left an impression on me. I was surrounded by people like my aunt who grappled with sadness but didn't lose their faith.

Why did you become a Dominican sister?

I really didn't want to! I was a shy girl. When I got into college, though, I wanted to go dancing and enjoy life; but something was always gnawing at me. Maybe I could help others to know that God loved them too? I wanted to get this idea of religious life out of my system and, without telling anyone, made an appointment to go to a distant convent to meet the Dominican prioress. She said to me, 'You can come, but it is going to be hard for you to leave your family.' But I felt I just had to try it. My parents were very surprised and had not expected it at all. As soon as I entered I really felt at home, and I loved the time to get to know God. I enjoyed the instructions and the studying of documents of the Vatican Council. I joined the Dominicans because they were the ones I knew, they were fun and joyful, and with them I could be myself. Of course, I missed not having my own family, but on the other hand, I was experiencing something that was more.

That sounds intriguing. What was 'more'?

The 'more' was an increased desire for God and an increased awareness of God's desire for me. This desire made other things relative. It was a longing connected with God and God's people. Even as I reflect on it now, I am amazed at how simple and joyful Dominican life was and still is. I wanted to be united with God and to be in a bigger world, to go beyond myself. But this was not the original direction that I had in mind for myself; I was led.

ON THE ROAD

Rome seems to have been an important step on your way. Why?

I first came to Rome as a theology student at the Angelicum
in the 70s, and I met people from all over the world. It was a
crossroads for me. When I returned to the United States years
later, there were movements among Dominican women, which
had started independently of each other in South Africa and in
Argentina, to establish international connections between us.
We didn't have any umbrella at that time, like the friars do, so
we wouldn't easily have known about Dominican congregations
in other countries who might have been in trouble, as the Iraqi
sisters were during the first invasion in Iraq.

   Thanks to the initiative of Timothy Radcliffe, we were invited
to Santa Sabina, the worldwide headquarters of the Order, in
Rome in 1995. We gathered sisters from all over the world and
we voted unanimously to form a movement to focus on our
charism as preachers and on justice and peace. We wanted to
form networks and never let any group be left alone, especially
during wars or struggles. I often say that, much like the founding
story of St Dominic who wept over the heretics in Southern
France, 'Out of the tears of the sisters of Iraq, Dominican Sisters
International (DSI) was born.' When I was elected as the first
international coordinator of DSI, I worked with different groups
in Europe, Asia and Africa, and it opened up an amazing world
to me!

You went 'on the road'. What did you see?

I went on a pilgrimage with other Dominicans to El Salvador
and Nicaragua during the wars in the 80s. I was shocked by
the poverty I saw. A Dominican friar who worked in a district
called Barrio 22 Aprile, on the outskirts of San Salvador, asked
me to join him to meet his parishioners. As we walked around,
I was stunned and started crying, because I couldn't believe
human beings could live in paper houses amid dust and squalor.
All of a sudden, a little girl, probably about 6 years old, dirty
and scantily dressed, comes running out of nowhere towards the
'padre'. As she hugged him, she saw me standing behind him, in

tears. She wiggled her way out of his arms, reached up, waved a hand to call me down so she could touch me; and she wiped away my tears. It was she who consoled me! I can still feel her touch; her hands were so dirty, but it didn't matter.

At the moment she hugged me, I realized that I was not just an American from Flatbush in Brooklyn, but a global citizen, and she was my little sister. That happened in 1987, and 25 years later I still remember her, and I am thankful for her and people like her who teach me about solidarity in the face of different economic situations. I have always looked for people who didn't speak my language or didn't think my way to find out about their hopes and dreams. It was that little girl on that rubbish heap that led me to discover my international vocation.

What did you learn from these experiences?

One thing I learned is that I can be weak and inept and still be happy. If you grow up in a culture like mine, you have to be educated, get a job, take care of yourself. I was used to being in charge as a teacher and an administrator, but as I went around the world, I saw people who were weak and who just had to cope with their limits and they were happy! I also noticed that, many times, the weak ones were daring. One can easily be misled into thinking that the courageous people are the strong ones, but I have seen the contrary.

COLLECTING ANTS

Are there visits you will always remember?

In 2009, I was in Zimbabwe and I saw sisters in impossible situations: violence, lack of food, assassinations. Yet they prayed the psalm 'Out of the depths, I cry to You'. While they knew the depths of human pain and trouble, they were full of confidence in God. They believed that God would care for them, and they felt that care expressed in their community. I was amazed because, if I had been in their situation, I would probably have given up. What I learned from them is the way they connected to one another within an extreme level of deprivation.

What about organizing a revolt instead of praying?

I have done that. I have taken strong stands and organized many protests, especially about the war in El Salvador in the 80s. But sometimes you have to find other ways. For example, in Zimbabwe I met the Shona people, who made change happen in a different way. The control by the government is so all-pervasive that, if they protest, they will be killed. So, they have to be creative and find other ways through networking and informing people on the outside.

What saddened you most?

In Harare, Zimbabwe, I was in a hospital visiting tuberculosis patients who didn't have sheets or medicines. There weren't even nurses or doctors! So, it was just a matter of dying. I was overcome with the sadness of it and went outside for a break when I noticed children taking twigs from a tree. They would wet the end of the twig, put it into a sand heap and then pull it up, catching ants. They would put them in a little container to take home. This was their families' supper! I was devastated.

Zimbabwe was once called 'the food basket of Africa', but people are starving now. Why did you go there?

I knew that the sisters were cut off and more or less alone. As we had promised when DSI was formed that we would never leave our sisters alone, I decided to go. It was at a time that President Mugabe didn't permit any visits because he blamed the West for the cholera problem. When I arrived, all the passports of the people in front of me were withheld, and they were put in jail. But I got in! The sisters were extremely thankful when they saw me. I wanted to wipe away their tears like that little girl had done for me in San Salvador.

In the face of death, deprivation and suffering, other ways to protest just have to be found. What kind of personal connection can I keep with the sisters? I hope to be able to offer education at our institutions in the United States, because these sisters rarely have the kinds of opportunities that we take for granted.

Where do you get your strength?

Seeing so many people in the midst of overwhelming obstacles who remain faithful and trusting in God no matter what, strengthens me. Another thing of tremendous importance is being in a community – my Dominican congregation has supported me all along the way. Finally, it is prayer that keeps me going. The experience of being with God and knowing that God is present in all these circumstances gives me courage. Whatever Gospel story we read, Jesus is always reaching out to the weak, the poor, the isolated and the marginalized. That call of compassion moves me to be with people in their struggles.

How do you pray?

Often, I pray with great difficulty because I am distracted; I have so much on my mind. We pray in the office and say the psalms morning and evening. Some of those psalms are very helpful like 'Why, oh God, have you forsaken me?'. Sometimes my prayer is demanding, like Catherine of Siena's in her intercessory prayer. I know God's love is merciful, but I often urge God to act. At other times, I really enjoy that loving glance, that contemplative experience that prompts me to respond in loving ways to God. A new way of prayer is prayer through peacefulness. I have been elected the Prioress of a new congregation, and we have 'Peace' as our name.

SEVEN IN ONE

Seven congregations have merged into the one of which you are the new Prioress. How do you look upon this new challenge?

Our new congregation has come from a number of years of reflection. One group had its original roots in Slovakia, another in Ireland, two in Germany and three in the United States. We have come together and adopted the name Dominican Sisters of Peace. The gift of peace is a great gift. It fascinates me that peace harmonizes truth so that we can have polarities and differences yet stay together.

We are over 600 Dominican sisters, and on the first anniversary of our new congregation, we also had 509 lay people making a commitment to collaborate with us in mission, which makes it very dynamic. We pray and study together, engage with ministries, help immigrants. We have three literacy centres, for example, which have over 40 different nationalities learning English.

As Prioress, I am the first among equals, and in that role I try to see what the members of our newly combined group have in common and how we can strengthen our unity for the sake of our mission. It's a challenge, indeed, but I welcome that.

ANTONIO DE MONTESINOS

Who is a source of inspiration to you?

Recently, I have been reading much about the 500th anniversary of the Spanish Dominicans who went to La Española (Haiti and the Dominican Republic). The Dominicans were sent by the Spanish throne to convert the indigenous people. When they got there, they realized that the indigenous people were being treated unjustly and that the very government that sent them had set up a labour system that was contrary to the Gospel. So they met in community, and they chose Antonio de Montesinos to give a homily. It was his famous sermon to the settlers on the fourth Sunday of Advent in 1511, and he said, 'Are they not human beings too? By what right and by which justice do you hold these Indians in horrible servitude? By what authority do you carry out such detestable wars against the peoples of the land?' After his speech, the Spanish government complained to the Dominican community about Montesinos, but all the friars stood behind their companion.

I am inspired anew by the boldness of that statement; by the way they took on the system. I asked myself why the Dominicans were different from the other Spaniards in La Española when they came out of the same culture and held the same values. I think the brethren were different because of their approach to the Indians: they befriended them.

But these are stories from the past. Can they still inspire today?

They do inspire me to look at how my American culture treats immigrants, treats the Earth. Our sisters in Iraq, in Zimbabwe and in so many countries defend marginalized people, whether they are Christians in Muslim countries or illegal immigrants in the States. These are not people from 500 years ago, these are people living now. Among our Dominicans in the US, three sisters went to prison for several years because they demonstrated against the US policy on weapons of mass destruction.

TO BE A PREACHER

Preaching is the core business of the Dominicans. What does it mean in your life?

Well, it has been a wonderful journey of discovery for me. My mother was a teacher, and I also became one. But I remember the shift when I realized that teaching is what I do, whereas being a preacher is who I am. As someone who announces the good news about Jesus Christ, I am reminded of St Francis of Assisi saying, 'Preach the Gospel at all times. If necessary, use words.' We have to be witnesses by the way we live, by treating other people fairly and by sharing our resources with those who are in need. Our retired sisters are still preaching without using words. It's a matter of identity for us. And of course, a preacher must be attentive to study. We cannot be consistently good preachers unless we continue to be students.

We are preachers, and we must have the courage to say difficult things; not in a harsh way, but in a way that the truth is heard. As Catherine of Siena said, 'Preach the Truth as if you had a million voices. It is silence that kills the world.'

8

Godfrey Nzamujo

PORTO NOVO, BENIN; INTERVIEW IN AMSTERDAM

Africans must come home

How do you start from scratch? Ask Godfrey Nzamujo, who kept asking the Benin government for a piece of wasteland that he could regenerate. To get rid of this persistent nuisance, the ministry allocated him one hectare of abandoned land. Nobody, except his own mother, believed that this young professor, who had studied in the USA, could make it work. Yet this proactive and determined man managed to develop the wilderness into an oasis, and so the Songhai project was born.

Nzamujo was named by his grandfather and he talks about his family with great love. They laid the foundation for his education, in which studying and taking responsibility were central.

He is an enthusiastic talker and highly energetic planner who spreads a good vibe around him. His laughter peals out as he tells me about the 'Sheraton Hotel for flies', explaining that everything is recycled at Songhai, even the intestines of animals! The only time he gets angry during our conversation is when he evokes those young Africans who go abroad to study and who don't return home to their own countries, but instead live a comfortable life in Europe or America. He calls them cowards!

This Dominican priest has been awarded many distinguished prizes and has received many honoured guests at Songhai, including Ban Ki-moon, the United Nations Secretary General, who described the project as an African centre of excellence.

Yet, when I ask about the most profound experience in his life, this fluent and articulate man grows almost silent. When the doctors wanted his pregnant mother to have an abortion, she ran away from home and gave birth to her son at great risk to her own life. The special bond between mother and child made him sense her dying moments when he was far away. He is moved to tears as he describes his affection for her: 'Because of her courage, I exist'!

> Godfrey Nzamujo was born in 1950 in Kano, Nigeria. He studied theology, philosophy and engineering, and lectured at the University of California Irvine and Loyola Marymount. When he returned to Africa, he set up the Songhai project in Porto Novo, Benin, and developed it into a pioneering farm, training and research centre. Under the motto 'Commitment to Excellence' the project has expanded to six sites in Benin and three in Nigeria. Father Nzamujo was awarded the Hunger Project's Africa Prize for Leadership in 1993 and is a member of the UN Independent Commission on Africa. In 2010, UN Secretary General Ban Ki-moon paid an appreciative visit to Songhai.

OUT OF AFRICA

Your parents valued education highly. Why was that?

My parents were involved in the medicine and real estate, but they were first of all strong Catholics who understood the value of education. From early on, they kept telling us that the only way to survive is to equip yourself intellectually, morally and spiritually. They used to say, 'If your name, your background, your money is taken away from you, you can still blossom because your education can't be nullified.'

The non-material force is what is most important in life. There is a saying in my homeland: 'Any child can eat with kings if he learns how to wash his hands.' If you prepare yourself through education, you wash your hands in a symbolic way and empower yourself. I never pray for the road ahead to be smooth, but I pray to develop the strength and skill to confront and navigate the hardships that come my way.

What is the meaning of your name?

In my ethnic group, every child gets his name from the situation at his birth. At the time I was born, my grandfather was in charge of land distribution. His own clan put pressure on him to distribute the land per head because it would favour his clan, but he refused and distributed it per family instead so that everybody was given fair treatment. As a result, he was heavily criticized. At my birth, he named me Nzamujo, meaning 'the hero cannot be intimidated'. In this way, my grandfather wanted to communicate to his people that he knew what he was doing and that he was doing it consciously.

When did you realize that the world was not as beautiful as you had expected as a child?

In the early 80s, during the big drought and famine in Africa, particularly in Ethiopia, I was working in my beautiful laboratory in California. When I saw these young Africans on television with swollen stomachs, I was appalled and wanted to return to Africa. My father, knowing I was romantic and idealistic, paid for my trip on condition that I looked around in Nigeria, South Africa, Kenya and Zaire. From the east to the west I saw beautiful rivers, I saw an Africa rich in opportunities, but I became terribly angry and frustrated because I wondered why such a rich continent should be so poor.

Did you find an answer?

I found a double answer: there is a structural problem and a problem of mentality. First, the wrong economic equation was written for Africa. This continent was designed to produce raw materials. It wasn't designed to be on the finishing line of production. *Development in the Western sense contributes to the African crisis by undermining the role of the native people.* Second, many Africans think that the solution to their problems is to be found in Europe instead of getting things going in Africa itself.

Do you have any bad childhood memories?

Not really.

You must! Nigeria is such a poor country.

It's a poor country, economically. I have lived in America and I have lived in Africa. My culture taught me to honour my parents and to serve the community and that's what brings joy. When I was on the road in Benin, I was looking for a place to sleep and a very poor family immediately offered me their bedroom. They knew that I was trying to start a project and lent me their bed as a sign of solidarity. I had the best bed in the house but I couldn't sleep. I got up in the night and saw their children sleeping on the floor, but what struck me was that they were resting so peacefully! A boy growing up in America is not as happy as these children. So, it's not the material things that make the difference.

So, why do many Africans want to come to Europe?

If you go to Europe to equip yourself and come back afterwards to build your nation, there's no problem. But thousands of Africans, the best we have, often settle in Europe to live a comfortable life. This angers me enormously.

When I was a student in America, I was president of the community of African black students and we invited Julius Nyerere, then president of Tanzania, for a meeting. He told us this story. There were two boys who went to school together. After graduation, each went his own way and when they met again after many years, one of them had become very rich while the other one hadn't. As the village of the rich man was far away, he said, 'Get me people so that we can transport food from my village to yours.' So, the poor man mobilized the strongest members of his community to transport the products. The local women, who were excited at the prospect of finally receiving provision for their children, gave these strong men the last bits of food they had and waited anxiously for their return. And they are still waiting… The students asked Nyerere, 'Who are those cowards?' He answered, 'It is you – educated Africans living out of Africa. You are the best we have and you won't use your intelligence for your own people!'

DOMINIC AND THOMAS

Who has inspired you?

St Dominic and St Thomas Aquinas themselves! First of all, I was inspired by the founder of the Dominicans because of his saying, 'Study, pray and share the fruit of it with your brothers in order to set them free.' Dominic came from a rich family, but when he saw the needs of his time he decided to empty himself so that he would be in a position to help. I was so impressed by his decision because it spoke to me. I had been growing up in Africa, studying in America and this man held a mirror up to my face! I understood that when you want to change people's lives, you have to become embedded in their reality and bring your own source of inspiration as well.

Can you give a concrete example?

St Dominic was ready to sell his books, his clothes, his furniture, even valuable manuscripts in order to help the poor with the money he received. The story goes that when his companions expressed astonishment that he should sell his books, Dominic replied, 'Would you have me study these dead skins when living skins, human beings, are dying of hunger?' I consider this a sign of nobility, of true aristocracy. He was ready to give up everything. It makes me think of the African proverb 'If you see what is bigger than the farm, you sell your barn.' The same is expressed in the parable in the Bible about a person who discovers a pearl in the field, sells everything and returns to buy the land. These stories all tell of the same universal experiences.

Why is Thomas Aquinas an example for you?

As a scientist, I was attracted to him because he wanted to use and integrate the best science of his time. I felt stimulated because I am trying to do the same thing at Songhai. Thomas understood that knowledge was liberating, whether through studying science or theology. Together with St Albert the Great, he was key to my choice of the Dominicans.

Unfortunately, I feel that present-day Thomism has lost the dynamics of its founder. This theological and philosophical system that dominated scholasticism has become fossilized. If St Thomas were to come back today, he would annihilate what has been made out of his theory. There is a remarkable story about St Thomas before he died. When he was celebrating Mass, he heard Jesus asking him what kind of favour he wanted. Thomas replied, 'Only you, Lord. Only you.' After this profound spiritual experience, he stopped writing. When he was asked to resume his work, he answered, 'I can't, because all that I have written seems like straw to me.' I think this story shows that he didn't want a big system to be made of his work. So, as a young Dominican, I opposed Thomism while admiring St Thomas for his emphasis on the flexibility of the human mind.

Why did you go to the United States?

I received a scholarship and was supported by the Dominicans. I studied theology, engineering and sciences at the same time. Some people thought this was an odd combination. I remember sitting an exam in Christology in the morning and one in electro-optical devices in the evening. It all belongs to the same field for me because it is the same 'me'. Reality is not engineering or science. Reality is about men and women, about the human drama, being part of a big whole. All those elements must coalesce to solve man's problems. That's why at Songhai we are creating a team of transversal, polyvalent young men and women who are looking at reality from many angles.

SONGHAI

What does 'Songhai' mean?

The Songhai Empire was one of the largest African empires in history. It existed between the fourteenth and sixteenth centuries and its name comes from its leading ethnic group, the Songhai. Its capital was the city of Gao where the Songhai had dwelt as a small ethnic group since the eleventh century. The clan grew into a big empire because of its ability to unite and engage with different people.

Where was it located?

It was in western Africa and covered what is now northern Nigeria, northern Togo, northern Ghana, northern Benin and all of Mali and Niger. The story goes that one of the emperors of Songhai went to Egypt, carrying so much gold that the economy was disrupted for months! Today, people don't know that there was a time when west Africa was immensely wealthy. We lost it all, but we can pick it up again. As I want to revive this old consciousness, I started using the name Songhai to make Africans aware that they came from an important culture.

How did the empire come to an end?

It was invaded by the Muslims and Moors from Morocco. The Songhai society, based on dialogue, was defeated by violence and fundamentalism. The empire was divided and some people were Islamized. The empire broke up into modern Mali, the Mandinka Empire and the Hausa-Fulani Empire. Some of those empires started breaking up internally. With the advent of Western colonialism and the slave trade, the dark ages of Africa set in.

What was your idea behind reviving Songhai?

The key question to me was: 'Can we develop a production system that corresponds to our African reality?' The technical competence I acquired in the United States and my faith were crucial in finding an answer to this question.

How would you define present-day Songhai?

It is an innovative, ecological agri-business centre providing a network of agricultural entrepreneurs with what Ban Ki-moon described as 'a spirit of self help'. But Songhai is not just about farming; it is about fighting poverty through education, by stimulating courage, taking responsibility and spreading family and community values.

What concrete steps did you take?

In 1985, I was given one hectare of wasteland in Ouando, a suburb of Porto Novo in Benin. It was a dumping site where not even weeds were growing. I had campaigned so hard to buy it that the government eventually gave in. I asked the Dominican sisters for some teenage dropouts to help me. During the dry season, we started irrigating, composting and cleaning the land. When the minister passed by and saw the progress, he was amazed. We produced our own fish and raised our own chicken and cows. Our success made people aware of their capacities.

To give you an example of the way I work, on Good Friday of Holy Week, I proposed not a procession through the streets to commemorate the stations of the cross but to dig a pond in the hot afternoon instead. That was our station of the cross! It caused a scandal, but I wanted to stress that the best way to honour the gift of God is to work. St Thomas Aquinas said 'We live well when we work well and do acts that overflow from our being.' We did exactly that in transforming this lifeless piece of land into a green, productive area.

BAN KI-MOON

What impressions do you retain from Ban Ki-moon's visit?

His visit in June 2010 came as a complete surprise. Benin's Minister of Foreign Affairs contacted me, saying, 'Ban Ki-moon is coming to Songhai. Get ready!' When we showed him the various projects, he was so impressed that he stayed longer than was officially foreseen. He visited everything! The production of our own energy, our livestock, our vegetables. He noticed the quality we produce, the prototypes we make. He said, 'I never thought I would see this type of thing.' He was so moved that he couldn't hide his feelings. Some of his assistants said, 'This is a man who doesn't easily show his emotions, but we can see that this really touches him.' His aides had prepared a speech for him but he put it aside and spoke from his heart. It happened to be his birthday and we had composed a song for him; there was a tremendously joyful atmosphere!

What elements were crucial to your success?

Again, my faith and the technical competence I acquired in the United States. The rest was a question of leadership and creating a culture of success. By starting small and making small successes, people started believing in themselves. It was marvellous to see the transition that took place in the young people!

We want to produce more with less. This is the basis of sustainability. In today's economy we produce more with more. We can't continue in this way.

What kind of projects have been created at Songhai?

We focus on agriculture, renewable energy, manufacturing and technical development. For example, solar panels power the internet café, scrap metal is welded into parts for machinery, IT instruction is provided. Our rice project is a tremendous success. We have created jobs at every level in the rice commodity chain. The blacksmiths are making the equipment for the parboiling, local women are organizing themselves into cooperatives, learning the skills of parboiling.

What do you recycle?

Everything! Waste from one sector is recycled and used as inputs for other sectors. Insects grown on leftovers from the restaurant, for example, feed fish cultivated in the aquaculture area. Aquatic plants help to filter our waste-water. Discarded coconut husks serve as a base on which to cultivate giant mushrooms.

It seems that even the intestines of animals are recycled!

There is a place we call Sheraton Hotel for the Flies. We chop the intestines into little pieces and add some bacteria to take away the smell. As a result, mosquitoes and malaria flies leave us alone! We use the eggs they lay there as larvae to feed our fish. This is called biomimicry, a discipline that examines nature – its models and systems – and then imitates these designs to solve human problems.

You must also have negative experiences at Songhai.

Yes. Most of the problems in development are caused by the people working in it. Projects often become ego trips. People tend to spend too much money on themselves, on conferences and travel, for instance. Songhai has stood against that in creating a culture of accountability. If you're given one penny, you have the moral obligation to multiply that money. In the Bible, the person that was given one penny and gave it back, was punished because he did not use it correctly. African leaders and people working in development who are stealing and embezzling money should realize that the resources don't belong to them!

THE LOST CONTINENT

Africa is often referred to as 'the lost continent'. What is your opinion?

I don't think Africa is lost. The media are creating a wrong image. They don't take the time to see the gem. Only yesterday, Europe was torn apart by war. How many millions of people were killed, only 60 years ago? Would you say Europe was lost? Look at the bloodshed in Ireland; look at Sarajevo; look at all the crises. When a woman is crying because she is in labour and it is difficult for the child to be born, do you say that it is a failure? No! We have to respect the period of gestation.

THE REAL ENEMIES

At Songhai, Muslims and Christians live together. How does it work?

I studied Islam to understand how to do deal with Muslims because we work together at Songhai. The real enemies are ignorance and poverty, not people or religions.

Do fundamentalist Muslims accept that ignorance is the problem?

Most of them do not, no, but we're breaking them down. During Ramadan, for example, I fast with Muslims and we get together in meetings. At first, they were surprised and worried, but I greeted them in Arabic, said some prayers with them and they started to look differently at me. One of the fundamentalists living here gets up at 5 in the morning to pray using loudspeakers so that everybody is woken up. I told him, 'Look, Prophet Muhammad would not do it this way. One mosque is not supposed to hear the other one.' He was surprised that I knew this recommendation and he turned his loudspeakers down the following week. We became friends and started a dialogue.

How many people from different faiths are there at Songhai?

We have Muslims, Christians, Evangelicals, Voodoo. Benin is the city of Voodoo, which is a traditionally recognized state religion.

Tell me your secret. How can all these religions live together peacefully?

It came from my upbringing. My father always told me to look at the good part of someone. In each of us there are two animals. The good, nice, gentle animal co-exists with a greedy, angry, negative one. Which animal will win depends on which you feed. I'm teaching my people that there is good and bad in a Christian, a Muslim, a Voodoo. And we emphasize spirituality, not religiosity. We ask what someone wants to contribute to Songhai.

CHUKU

Is Mass celebrated differently from in Europe?

Mass in Benin rocks! It is so beautiful. Our people enjoy coming here because it strikes an answering chord to their questions. When I say Mass, the bread is the combination of the gifts of the sun, the water and the soil. The wine is the pain and anguish coming from the grapes that have to be crushed, but it becomes a symbol of friendship!

Who is God to you?

Don't define God! When you start defining God, you've lost Him. In my culture, the supreme deity of Eastern Nigeria is called Chuku, meaning 'great spirit'. The traditional theology of my people stresses the fact that you don't define God because He is self-evident. He is within you, not outside.

What experience has changed your life?

The experience of being lost when my mother died a few years ago. I was very close to her because I was a premature child. The doctors had told her she would die if she tried to keep her baby. But she ran away on the day they came to perform the abortion. I exist today because of her courage! From the beginning, the bond was there.

I wasn't present when my mother died, but I had a very strong feeling that something was wrong a few hours before her death. I had phoned my brothers but nothing seemed to be wrong. Nevertheless, after a few hours I got a call telling me she was dead. I had already sensed that my mother was gone. At the moment of her death, something was communicated. When I finally reached her house, she was lying on her bed. I just stood there and cried my soul out. Even though she was dead, I had a strong feeling of connectedness, of God's presence through that bond. Each time I feel exhausted and I revisit that experience, I feel my mother hasn't left me. When I was trying to start this project, nobody believed in it, but she said, 'My son, go. You'll succeed!'

I succeeded. My priesthood is in line with her way of life. The day I announced I was going to be a Dominican priest, nobody believed it because I was a bit of a rascal, but my mother said, 'I knew you would become a priest, and you knew it yourself.' A spiritual experience can't be proven intellectually; it is the heart speaking. I was able to work for others because my mother was ready to sacrifice her life for me.

What did you think when you were at her deathbed?

I went through all the things we had lived together. We used to pray the rosary together. I was overwhelmed when I found out that she died clutching the rosary I had given her.

A TIME TO BE BORN

Why are you optimistic about Africa's future?

Man is capable of both good and bad. Christ was disgraced on

Good Friday, but the beauty of the resurrection came after the ignominy of His death on the cross. What attracted me to the Dominicans was their presence in places where there is suffering, where Good Friday is lived. Wherever there is human drama, you'll find Dominicans.

There is nothing permanent in our life. There is a time to be born and a time to die, because that is nature. Africa may seem to be on the losing side for the time being, but honestly, from what I feel, from what I see, tomorrow is African time.

9

Timothy Radcliffe

BRUSSELS, SPRING 2009

An itinerant preacher

Some ten years on, Timothy Radcliffe and I meet again in Brussels. When we had our first interview in the Santa Sabina Priory, an impressive building on the Aventine in Rome, I was surprised by his enthusiasm and lack of formality. I followed him over the years and read the books he wrote. He was the youngest and most unconventional Master of the Order I had seen, joking about his portrait, which one day would hang in the Dominican portrait gallery. That day came in 2001 when his term ended.

I ask him if he misses the Santa Sabina. He weighs his answer: yes and no. They were nine happy years, but it was enough. Now he can go to Rome occasionally without having to worry about letters waiting to be answered. He is as cheerful as ever and still looks his usual, boyish self, with tousled hair and rumpled habit. He has kept travelling and meeting with his 'brothers and sisters', as he so affectionately calls his community.

Ten years ago, we talked about the most important word for him: *veritas*, 'truth'. This time, we focus on questions of the day: Islam, identity, sexuality. Although he is very shy about his aristocratic roots, I am allowed a glimpse of what that kind of upbringing meant 60 years ago. The whole family was dressed formally for dinner which took place in an atmosphere of ritual courtesy. I get the impression of his childhood as if plucked from an English period novel, inhabited by lords and ladies. But the story he tells me takes an unexpected turn. When his father's firm closed down, he was so concerned about his former employees that he paid them their full wages until each of them found a new job. It practically ruined the family, but it shows in what kind of environment young Timothy was raised.

He speaks lovingly of his parents, and especially his mother who once took him as a small boy to the Dominican church in Oxford, as she held its founder, Bede Jarrett, in great admiration. A forerunner to his later vocation? Blackfriars would indeed become Timothy's home and place to travel from as an itinerant teacher.

GEOLOGICAL PATIENCE

As Master of the Order from 1992 to 2001, you travelled extensively, and you have continued to do so, which means that you draw on an exceptionally wide ministry. Have you noticed new questions emerging over the years?

When I began to travel, some 20 years ago, we were dominated by the question of the confrontation between East and West, capitalism versus Communism. Now there are two big questions. One is ecology, because we are only beginning to understand the importance of living sustainably. And the second is the relationship with Islam. In almost every country where I travel, I see people trying to establish friendship with Islam.

Isn't it a rather one-sided friendship? I just talked with Monseigneur Teissier, Emeritus Archbishop of Algiers, about this issue. In 2006, a regulation was passed in Algeria which prohibited Muslims from converting to Christianity.

It varies depending on where you are. We often confuse Islam with the culture of a particular country. In the Maghreb, in North Africa, for example, the situation is entirely different from Indonesia where there is a form of Islam much more open to dialogue. The first thing you have to do is show respect. The famous Egyptian Dominican, Anawati, who began a dialogue with Islam 50 years ago, said that you need 'geological patience'. If you can achieve friendship, then you have the basis for dialogue.

Muslims are building mosques in Western Europe, but the Orthodox Christians in Turkey are not even allowed to reopen their schools.

That's a big problem and it's quite right that we insist on reciprocity. Otherwise, we are not caring for the Christian minorities in Islamic countries. But we have to understand why many Muslims are very critical of the Western culture. On the one hand, Western culture has a wonderful freedom, a beautiful tolerance, which I love, and a lot of creativity in films and novels and music, for example. On the other hand, it is a culture which has lost its moral vision. Seeing everything in terms of the market can be degrading. So I can understand a Muslim reaction to that.

We have to mediate between the many Muslims in our Western countries and our culture. Unfortunately, it is always tempting to find an enemy and I don't think it is entirely an accident that when Communism disappeared as 'the enemy', we found Islam. So I think we project a lot of fears onto Islam.

On the other hand, Muslims were behind the 9/11 attacks.

Yes, that is true and it is also true that some followers of Islam are very militant and aggressive and want the war against the West. But we are not going to help if we simply identify Islam as the enemy. The vast majority of Muslims are opposed to terrorism and want to become good citizens of our countries.

Do we need an enemy?

Well, nearly all societies look for an enemy. Before Communism, for centuries, Islam was seen as Europe's enemy. The Muslim invasion of North Africa, which had been Christian for centuries, and then the conquest of Spain and the advance as far as Vienna meant that for much of European history, Islam was seen as an external 'enemy'. After the brief interruption of Communism, we have returned to what is a very old perception of Islam. But now very often Islam is also seen as the enemy within.

This is dangerous and unjust. We have to discover a secure enough identity, a sense of community that does not depend upon uniting against an enemy. The heart of Christianity is the belief that Jesus was the innocent scapegoat on whom everything was loaded. The French philosopher René Girard has shown that it is a universal temptation to find a scapegoat and kill it. There are indeed parts of Islam like Wahhabism that are very anti-western. But to regard that as the whole of Islam would be untrue and disastrous.

IDENTITY

You point out that one way to cope with this problem is to strengthen our identity. What do you mean? Our identity as Christians, as Westerners, as atheists...?

I think there are several elements here. Let me take the example of English identity. What does it mean for me to be English? In the past, we often had an identity linked with conquest: conquering the Scots, the Irish, the Welsh and then as much of the world as we could get hold of! It was a very militaristic identity. Now that the days of empire are gone, the challenge is how to have an identity rooted in a cultural tradition: poetry and music for instance. I also hope we, in England, would discover who we are by a certain sort of hospitality to strangers.

What is your identity?

Mine? Well, much of my life has been about losing identity. My family comes from Yorkshire. About 30 years ago, the old family home, Rudding Park, was sold and is now a luxury hotel and golf course. I was sad when it was sold because we had been there for almost 200 years, but we had to let it go. When I joined the Order I had to, in a sense, let go of that rather exclusive identity to discover a new broader one, as the brother of all sorts of people in the Order, and gain a new sense of being British. When I went to Rome and travelled all around the world, I had to discover a new identity again, with brothers and sisters in every country of the planet. In Christ, I am on the way to finding myself as a member of the whole human family, an identity that is not defined over anyone! A full sense of who we are always lies in the future.

Barack Obama, for example, is very interesting. He is trying to find an identity as someone who is black but who is not anti-white. In the United States, how can he have an identity built on not being white? His book *Dreams From My Father* is a beautiful, intelligent exploration of that.

It seems that you grew up in two rigidly hierarchical institutions – the English aristocracy and the Catholic Church. How do you view the class-divided society of England?

In England today, in all honesty, your social background is much less important.

But not when you grew up.

Not when I grew up, no.

You come from an English aristocratic family.

You could say that, yes.

Wasn't there a story about a car...?

When I was staying at my uncle's (he had a very big country house with lots of bedrooms), he asked me when my train to Oxford was, but I said I was going to hitch-hike, which he thought was scandalous. In the end, his chauffeur delivered me in the Rolls Royce to a spot on the road where I could start hitch-hiking and I got a lift in a lorry! That is a wonderful liberation, isn't it?

But you could have led a very easy life!

When I first joined the Order, it was a bit difficult because I had never lived closely with people from a different background. I think they found me a bit odd and I probably found them a bit odd. But within a month that was finished.

One of the things that attracted me to the Order was that it is classless. In England, the class system was a bit oppressive. One of the attractive things about becoming a Dominican was entering a spacious area where anybody could be your friend.

The other aspect of your identity is being a Catholic. How do you see the hierarchical aspect of Catholicism?

You could imagine the Church like a bus. To hold the bus together, you need a chassis. It's the rigid bit underneath that holds the engine and all the seats and everything in place. Without the chassis, the bus will come to pieces. But the most interesting thing is not the chassis; it is where you travel, who you travel with, what you see. It's the adventure of the journey.

In the Church, the hierarchy is a bit like the chassis. You need it to hold the church together, but it's not very interesting. The interesting thing about being a Catholic is not the hierarchy, but discovering the Gospel, the wonders of the love of God, love of the stranger, love of yourself. It's discovering freedom. These are the important things about the Church.

But what do you tell people who feel oppressed by the decisions made by the hierarchy?

First of all, we must have confidence to discuss these issues and second, we often underestimate the extent to which members of the hierarchy are open to dialogue. Let us talk and seek new ways together.

THE CLOSER YOU GET, THE LESS YOU SEE

Did your image of God change while you were Master of the Order?

I think that one gradually loses images of God. When I was a child, I thought God had a nice white beard and sat on a throne. I was wrong! As a young friar, I thought God was a very powerful person. Again, I had to lose that image. This is called the *via negativa*. It's like kissing somebody: the closer you get, the less you see. When you do kiss somebody, you don't see anything at all! In the spiritual life, you let go of one image after another until you see nothing.

Isn't that a kind of void? Can't it be depressing?

No. Not at all; quite the opposite. If you get close to God, you will see things through God's eyes, just as we are intimate to a friend by seeing things together rather than just looking at each other. When Thomas Merton, after ten years in the monastery, had to leave to get a little pamphlet printed, he was struck by the goodness of everyone he saw! God says to every human being what He said to His son: 'It's wonderful that you exist.' We are close to God when we share His delight in others.

How do you become close to God?

Well, just like you come close to anyone. First of all you have to spend time with Him. You have to learn to listen. If you have a deep friendship with anyone, it means you hear what they are saying, not what you think they ought to be saying.

Can you really hear what God is saying? How do you know you aren't deceiving yourself?

It's not as if suddenly my mobile phone goes off and God is on the line. I don't literally hear God say anything to me; but I discover who I am when I read the scriptures because I discover the story of my life; the story that makes sense of my happiness, my sorrow, my success, my failure. It's about identity.

You asked me about my childhood and my joining the Dominicans and I told you the story of my life. But when I pick up the Bible I discover a story of God's relationship with humanity and I recognize my own story. When I read the Gospel, I find myself inside the story. I am the Samaritan woman, the man born blind, the leper, Peter... The excitement of reading the scriptures is that you are always inside that encounter. So, hearing God includes discovering a quite new sense of who I am, just as when you love someone, you discover who you are with them.

Are youngsters still interested in these stories?

Oh yes, absolutely. Youngsters have the same struggles and share the same humanity. These stories have been interesting for 2000 years.

IN THIS WORLD OR THE NEXT

What do you perceive as being the greatest needs of youngsters?

The big questions are about hope because young people see a future that is economically uncertain and they fear for the future of the planet. We have an enormous challenge of ecological catastrophe. The lives of millions of people are at risk.

So how can you talk about hope?

That's *the* question isn't it? We have no more knowledge of what is going to happen than anyone else, but we believe God creates no one in vain. God creates every human being for happiness, and we will attain that happiness in this world or the next.

How do you know?

I believe. I've already seen that happiness, that deep joy in so many people who know that they are made for happiness.

What else do youngsters look for?

In my experience, they look first of all for authenticity – a very important word! They expect that if we have doubts, we express them and when we have convictions, we speak them.

The second thing they look for is freedom. The Church very often gives the impression of not saying what it really thinks. But we are no witness to Christ unless we are authentic, free and joyful. But the joy is not a happy-clappy charismatic joy. On the contrary, it's a joy that is big enough to embrace sorrow; otherwise, it is not authentic.

THE HEART OF SEXUALITY

One of the delicate areas for young people is sex. Do you get questions about it?

I had a wonderful evening in a disco in Singapore, in which I was interviewed by a young Indonesian Franciscan. We had a good time, the place was absolutely filled, and near the end they all wanted to talk about sex! (*Laughs*)

What did they want to know?

They often want to know what is allowed and what is forbidden. But you can't understand sexuality by looking at rules. You have to understand the beauty of sexuality. The best starting point is the Last Supper, when Jesus says, 'This is my body and I give it to you.' At the heart of sexual ethics, two people say to each other, 'I give myself to you.'

This makes you very vulnerable. Jesus put Himself in the disciples' hands, vulnerable to whatever they would do to Him. And one of them betrayed Him, another denied Him, and most of the rest ran away. So if you give your body to another, then that means vulnerability, as well as generosity and fidelity. Jesus gave Himself to us forever.

You point out that our society trivializes the body and reduces it to an object we can own. Why is this view damaging?

If the body is just something I own like a mobile phone or a car, my body is degraded. You can give a laptop and remain yourself, but if you give your body to somebody, you give yourself and so are changed.

Unfortunately the temptation in our culture is to see so many things in terms of property. As early as in the seventeenth century, the body is considered a property, and then the body of the wife is seen as the property of the husband. Much of European law is founded on the assumption that the wife belongs to the husband as disposable property. That's a terrible foundation to your relationship with another human being.

Our culture seems to encourage people to promiscuity. What's wrong with that?

If you sleep around, then you are undermining your ability to give yourself fully, generously and faithfully to someone. But it would be a mistake to walk in a room and say, 'I understand there is a lot of promiscuity going on here and it must stop!' You have to accompany youngsters on their path and the moment will come when they want to ask fundamental questions.

Another thing you point out is the dualism between body and soul. You say it is not a Christian concept, whereas popular opinion often holds the opposite.

In Western culture, long before Christianity, there was a tendency towards dualism. It was already present in the time of Plato hundreds of years before Christianity. In the second century, Christianity opposed the dualism of Gnosticism. The Manicheans in the fourth century and the Albigensians in the thirteenth century were advocating dualism once again. Descartes in the seventeenth was tempted by the dualism of mind and body. Much scientific thought today is dualistic. So I think there has been a constant tendency in the West towards dualism.

Christianity has often tried to resist it but sometimes failed. One of the fascinating things about Thomas Aquinas, for example, is his insistence on the complete unity of body and soul. Aquinas had an extraordinary vision of the radical unity of the human person.

St John of Damascus preached about the sacredness of sex. Isn't that unbelievable for a Christian saint?

I hope not. The Song of Songs in the Bible is very erotic. In the first encyclical of the Pope's *Deus caritas est*, you can read that the Pope insists on the unity of erotic love and Christian love. He says they are one love. One of the reasons why people trivialize sex nowadays is that they take the erotic out of it, so it becomes mechanical and impersonal, something like cleaning your teeth.

But negative ideas about sexuality did pervade Christianity, didn't they?

It's a complicated story; but just one example: in the Middle Ages you don't find so much negative teaching about sex. In Dante's *Divine Comedy*, the sexual sins were seen as less grave than, for example, telling lies or betraying friends, because people are seeking a good, but in the wrong way. After the Enlightenment, suspicion of sex becomes more prominent.

THE TRINITY

You expressed your belief in the Trinity. Isn't it a rather abstract concept?

No, not at all. The belief in the Trinity is one of the most exciting down-to-earth beliefs there is. It principally looks at two things. In Jesus Christ, we don't meet a theory about God or a messenger from God, but God in person. God is present to us with a human face. The second thing is that in the Trinity we find a love that is equal, without domination or manipulation. It's a love that always lifts us into equality. We don't often love one another as equals. We may have a condescending, patronizing love or we may love somebody as a wonderful hero above us. What we see in the Trinity is that true love brings us towards equality.

The topic seems to have disappeared from the pulpit. I haven't heard a good homily about the Trinity for quite a while.

I think that's part of a larger problem which is that we often think of spirituality as nice and warm and doctrine as arrogant, abstract and incomprehensible. But doctrine is exciting and liberating. When you get involved with the Christian doctrines – the resurrection, the Trinity, the divinity of Christ – you are invited on an adventure in the discovery of the truth. Doctrines don't close our minds, they open them. I think it's unfair to young people to give them just a nice vague spirituality. It's boring.

But what about Eucharist? Isn't that boring too?

It often is. It is often badly celebrated with terrible music and unbelievably bad sermons. But, it is the moment that Jesus gives Himself to us in His body and blood. We may not know how to celebrate the gift well, but at the essence of the Eucharist, Jesus says, 'I give myself to you.' How could one not say yes? What could be more wonderful?

I see a lot of people who don't say yes and stay in bed on Sunday mornings.

Some people probably see Eucharist as an obligatory ritual rather than as a wonderful gift. Compare it to getting a phone call on a cold morning from your girlfriend who has a wonderful gift for you and asks you to come. Even if the journey is boring, you still go because you want to receive this gift. The most important thing of all religion is its gift.

PRAYERS AND CROSSES

How do you pray?

How do you talk to your husband? People have many different forms of conversation with their husbands or their wives. Sometimes they will joke, sometimes they will discuss the news or talk about their plans for the future or quarrel. It's the same in our relationship with God. Sometimes you pray in silence or you sit with the people you love in silence, sometimes you read or listen to what they're saying to you and sometimes you may be having an argument with God. I think that's fine too. In Judaism, there's a strong tradition of getting angry with God. You need all of these forms of communication with God.

In your book Seven Last Words, you refer to the crosses you received from people on your journeys. Which is your favourite?

The one I love most is from Haiti. It shows a peasant on pilgrimage. It is dark, but he's walking towards the sun. It reminds me of my own travels: often at night, getting stuck at an airport because they have cancelled the plane and I wonder where I am going, what I am doing. This cross shows that there is always a path; there is always light in the end.

10

Helen Alford

The best kept secret of the Church

Helen Alford is teaching in one of the most beautiful buildings in Rome. She is the first woman to be Dean of the social sciences faculty of the Dominican University in Rome – the Angelicum, named after 'the Angelic Doctor', Thomas Aquinas.

Sister Helen Alford is self-confident without trumpeting her high-ranking position in one of the city's major pontifical universities. She welcomes me warmly and shows me around the university, which was built at the end of the sixteenth century as a monastery for nuns. The nuns moved out during the 1930s, and the professors moved in. The nuns' cells on the first floor are now occupied by the lecturers, who are mostly Dominican friars.

During our interview, sitting on a bench in the cloister, students enter and leave the ground-floor classrooms. They gather round the fountain in the middle of this courtyard to talk. 'Nearly 100 different nations are represented here across social and language barriers. It's a much broader form of learning than you could find elsewhere,' sister Helen explains.

As she shows me around the chapel, she draws my attention to the paintings. The Dominican nuns who lived here in the monastery's early days must have been self-conscious women! They didn't like the idea of the Virgin Mary favouring St Dominic above St Catherine of Siena (as suggested by traditional paintings depicting her giving a rosary to St Dominic). So these nuns commissioned the painter to have the Virgin give the rosary to St Catherine instead. On a painting of Heaven and Hell, all the Dominican nuns appear in Heaven, while Hell is reserved for others!

Is the Church's social teaching its best kept secret? Not when you hear Sister Helen enthusiastically and fluently holding forth about encyclicals, papal documents, trade unions and private property, and then mentioning a Dominican Nobel prize winner (Dominic Pire). Listening to this Dominican expert is like reading a thrilling novel set in a mysterious Vatican university.

Helen Alford was born in South Croydon in 1964 and studied engineering at Cambridge University. She is Dean of social sciences at the Angelicum, the pontifical university of the Dominicans in Rome. She has co-authored and co-edited several books, of which *Managing as if Faith Mattered* is a kind of forerunner to the papal encyclical about ethics and religion in business.

PUSHING AT AN OPEN DOOR

Isn't the Church's social teaching perceived as dull?

Thirty years ago, there were a lot of inspirational movements that focused on social issues. But there is a transformation going on and those movements are going through that as well. Nevertheless, I feel our work here to be all the more important because we are trying to help that transition to a new face. It is important that we stick to our guns and carry on that tradition in order to make it available as a resource for future generations, so that they can use it in a way that's relevant to society.

Did you have to fight your way to the top of a pontifical university?

It was a very happy day for me when I was elected Dean, but being a woman posed no problem. The Angelicum is a pontifical university and its statutes come from the Vatican, but the Dominicans are pretty independent in how they run the university. Because the Order has been open to men and women from the beginning, the idea of a woman in that position was kind of pushing against an open door. Although until I came along it had always been held by a man.

Did you get any comments about your position?

The younger generations don't see it as such a big deal; they just work with me. Some people have expressed their hope that this would mark the beginning of a new period in terms of Vatican structures. There is no doubt that there is more room for women in the Vatican and in the pontifical universities nowadays.

Part of the problem is that the orders have usually been the ones running the universities and they are no longer in a very strong position, as they don't have many vocations. There may be a lot of women out there, but they may not be able to access a position like mine because they are not members of an order. Our university is run by the Dominican Order, so to be Dean you have to be a Dominican.

Nevertheless, it is an important sign!

You are absolutely right. When we organized a course on the social teaching of John Paul II, my lecture dealt with one of his social encyclicals and I picked out what he said about women and work. I was surprised to find that many of the students selected this very item for their paper afterwards. African priests, for instance, wrote about the discrimination against their sisters, mothers and members of their parishes and they considered this point important for their diocese and their country.

Do you have to be a feminist to get into this high position?

You have to have confidence in what women can do. The word 'feminist' is a bit loaded. I try to stay away from words like that because they can be off-putting, which is no good for winning over your audience. We need more role models and we have to relate to all the different social situations because we are an international university. I am playing a role that would be normal for a woman in the West, and for the sisters and lay women from India or other countries my position can be an inspiration and an encouragement to have more confidence in themselves. From my experience, the priests and the ecclesiastical structures in those countries are helping women and not holding them back.

CATHERINE OF SIENA

Is Catherine of Siena important to you?

Certainly. She was such an inspiring woman, who talked about politics and international relations in the fourteenth century. This woman managed to bring the papacy back to Rome from its displacement in France. She was proclaimed a Doctor of the Church in 1970 and she became one of the two patron saints of Italy, together with Francis of Assisi. Her ability to bring about real change was amazing.

Why did people listen to her?

She was so obviously inspired by the love of God. She was not trying to promote her own case, even though as a result of what she did, she became one of the most famous women in the history of the Church. Catherine was utterly dedicated to trying to bring about reform in the Church, to getting the papacy to really live up to its vocation at a time when it was not at its best.

What images did she use?

There is a wonderful long text called *The Dialogue* in which she is talking to God. Through the incarnation, God entered into human life and Jesus built a bridge to help us come back to God. In this striking image, Jesus himself constructs this bridge using His own blood to make the cement. It's not the sort of image that you would expect from a medieval woman; it makes me think of modern art instead. This idea of bridge-building is very powerful because we are living in a fragmented society. On the one hand, such a society can provide freedom, but on the other, there is also a very negative aspect because we lose communication with each other. So, creating a bridge among each other and towards God is a very powerful image.

A LITTLE BIT TOO FAR

You studied engineering at Cambridge. Isn't that a man's world?

Well, most of the students were men, but nobody made a

comment about me studying in that field. I was interested in sciences at school, but I wanted to do something more practical and so chose engineering. While studying, I became interested in human beings working in technical systems, so I started thinking about how we interact with technology.

Were you already a Dominican sister?

No, not at that stage. In fact, the experience of studying those subjects helped me move towards the Dominicans. I was in a department where we were encouraged to listen to different ideas. When I told my father I wanted to work on a thesis on human work in computer-integrated manufacturing systems, he advised me to read Leo XIII's *Rerum Novarum*. I had never heard of this encyclical before, but my father, who is a convert, encouraged me. I founded my thesis on Catholic social thought, intrigued by the question of what is the right way to treat human beings in modern systems.

The other people in the department found this just a bit too religious. They stopped talking to me about it, although they never told me I should drop the subject. When I got to the defence of my thesis, something odd happened. When it came to the chapter about social doctrine, the two examiners, who had obviously read all of it, just turned it over and said, 'Well, your position in Chapter 2 is very interesting, but it's held by a very small number of people.' Which was their way of saying, 'We don't have to look at it or ask questions about it.' Of course, if I had had more courage at that point, I would have challenged their view, because the world's Christian/Catholic population isn't a small number of people – although they may be fewer in British universities...

At the same time, I started frequenting a Dominican house, where I could discuss this connection, as well as all my other points of view. The Dominicans were clearly broad-minded and, as they had lay people staying with them, I visited them often and began exploring the possibility of becoming a Dominican. If I hadn't had the experience of studying these subjects and talking with the Dominicans, I'm not sure I would have arrived at the decision to join them.

Why does the Church have a social doctrine?

Ultimately, it stems from the Incarnation. God entered our world, and so what happens in our world is important. Since the earliest times there has been reflection on what is the right and the wrong thing to do and how we should live in our society. The nineteenth century was a time of intense social change: industrialization, the growth of capitalism, the rise of the nation state in Europe.

This brought the Church's reflection to a new level, and this is where the idea of social teaching really took off. The Church was responding to the same kind of social problems as sociology, psychology and all those other modern disciplines seek to do.

The official teaching started in 1891 with Pope Leo XIII's encyclical called *Rerum Novarum*, in which the Pope was concerned about working people. The encyclical caused a big stir at the time, because of its emphasis on the need to respect workers' rights.

Why did that cause a big stir?

Because it seemed so close to what the socialists and more left-wing people were saying. After the French revolution, the Church was seen very much as a right-wing organization defending the conservative view. So this document added another dimension to what the Church was teaching.

However, it also challenged socialism, because one of the things the Pope really stressed was the importance of property. He insisted that everyone needed to have something he could call his own on the basis of which to found a solid life, a family and security for children.

Most meaningful was his defence of working people against the more powerful groups in society that had risen with the advent of capitalism and industrialization. *Rerum Novarum* gave a big boost to the nascent trade unions that were influenced by priests and Catholic thinkers, and support for working people became an issue. For instance, some of the Dominicans at that time started studying modern social disciplines like sociology, so as to be better able to help workers and understand their problems.

Another formative moment came with *Populorum Progressio*, the 1967 encyclical by Pope Paul VI on the development of peoples. The key idea here is that we should be concerned about the world as a single social system. It is not only the workers we see around us who deserve our solidarity, but the whole of the human family. The Church must be behind all that's good in terms of human development in general throughout the world.

Are people aware of the Church's concern for working people?

More is happening than actually gets communicated through media channels, partly because people don't want to blow their own trumpets, although maybe they should! Things are getting done, but quietly. Another example is the fact that 20 to 30 per cent of AIDS care worldwide is provided by Catholic or Christian organizations, which is now recognized by the UN, but may not otherwise be well-known.

Do you see an evolution in the debate about the Church's social teaching?

Certainly. Three years ago, I co-edited a book about the Dominicans' contributions to social ethics in the twentieth century, titled *Preaching Justice*. We found that the whole idea of social teaching is about being in dialogue with what is happening in the world. A perfect example of this is given by the Belgian Dominican Dominique Pire who won the Nobel peace prize in 1958. Let me quote (*Preaching Justice*, p.141) something from him about dialogue:

To dialogue means to look beyond the boundaries of one's conviction for the duration of the dialogue so as to share the heart and spirit of the other, without abandoning any part of one's self in order to understand, judge and appreciate the real goodness and usefulness present in the thoughts, feelings and actions of the other. One must really feel oneself with the other. It therefore requires one to bracket off one's self for a moment, who we are and what we think, so as to understand and appreciate the other positively without necessarily sharing the other's point of view. In this there is a profound renunciation of self.

In the 1920s, totalitarian systems were much debated. During the War, questions of peace arose. In the 50s and 60s, development was a huge subject. Nowadays, the big issues are environment, human trafficking and the economic crisis. In our teaching, we try to react to current problems.

For example?

The current Pope's statement, towards the end of his first social encyclical, about the need for a new form of world governance has been picked up by a lot of people. He stressed that we need to find 'fraternity in the economy'. The economy isn't just a place of pure exchange; it should be a place where we can develop more fully as human beings.

A RETHINK

Social justice issues are often seen as belonging to the political left. Correct?

We have to try to confront social problems through politics, and it is true that in recent history the parties that have often been more willing to listen to questions of social justice have been on the left. But we are currently seeing a transformation in politics. Young people think less in terms of the right-left divide. That division belongs to a particular world view that sees human freedom as an ultimate goal. The socialists have emphasized redistribution of wealth as a condition for freedom, but they basically agree with those of a more liberal leaning that the central point is human freedom. What is becoming a much more active issue now is the question of how spirituality and religion connect to politics.

God and business: what does one have to do with the other?

You always have to remember that a business is not a machine for making money; it is people that make a business work.

But business managers only want to make profits and satisfy shareholders!

Managers have often been taught in business schools to maximize shareholder profits, but many business people have problems with that idea because in working with others, relationships are developed. Why do people feel bad when somebody is laid off? From a purely technical perspective, they would be saving money. But people don't just have a purely economic relationship with each other, there is more to it – a sense of person and family, for example. These normal human reactions should be a part of business life. There is a rethinking going on in the business disciplines. If you consider that our big business leaders have all gone through courses on business ethics, we can ask ourselves how much universities are also responsible for the economic crisis.

How do you judge the importance of businesses in our world?

We all know what societies are like that don't have enough economic activity. People don't want to live in them. That's one reason why we have so much migration to Europe.

Businesses are making a real contribution to a just human social order. But once companies become very big, they tend to become disconnected from a social community and the danger then emerges that people become purely financially focused. That has to be challenged.

Why do we work? Why do we go into business? If earning a living is the only answer, you can easily feel unfulfilled. Business is ultimately about creating a better human society. If we don't come back to this idea when training people in business schools, we undermine the legitimacy of business and end up with an economic crisis.

AS IF FAITH MATTERED

Does faith really matter in business, as you suggest in Managing as if Faith Mattered?

There is the beginning of an awakening among business people, but it is not yet broadly felt. If you go to the European Academy of Business in Society, however, they will listen to your arguments. Where do people get their ideas regarding the right way to behave? Many derive it from their religious convictions. If we don't allow people to bring that conviction to their work, in a very simple, non-triumphalist way, we are cutting off resources that can make our businesses work better.

What does faith have to do with business?

If I do have some kind of faith, I don't just leave it outside the door when I go into my workplace. One of the problems is that people don't feel able to bring their moral tradition into their work, so they tend to do things they would never do at home.

For instance?

Well, treating people in a way that is demeaning; creating work systems that don't allow people to develop; polluting the environment. Rich people don't want to live in places where there are lots of factories because the environment is bad.

Is it possible to unite your faith with your working discipline?

There are always going to be differences between what you do in your family and what you do at work. That's normal because home and work are different contexts that deal with different problems. But it is more difficult to split your personality when it comes to deciding what is the right thing to do. If you justify to yourself doing something in the workplace that you would never do in another context because you consider it to be wrong, then you start to have a breakdown in your life. It's that kind of splitting which is a problem.

We are searching for meaning in what we are doing. More and more people in the business world are recognizing that there is more than the technical side to our work. Bringing more of our humanity and our faith into our work could help solve the problem. I'm not talking about forcing a particular faith; we have to have an interreligious dialogue that is compatible with a multicultural society.

Aren't you too optimistic?

You have to give people a vision of what new business models could be like. This is both realistic and beyond realism; prophetic and visionary. Our job at the university is to help people embrace a vision of such new models because we have to change the way businesses are run. We have to be more socially sustainable in terms of work-life balance.

AEROSPACE

You worked in cellular manufacturing in an aerospace company. What was your experience?

I was interested in the question of human work in high-tech systems. I got the chance to work with the British Aerospace on the reorganization of their production system. I was assigned to the component area that produced the doors, parts of the wings and so on. I helped to set up the 'cells' and monitored their progress.

The idea of the cell was to create a small, relatively independent manufacturing unit in which the workers themselves could control the flow of products in and out. They controlled their own quality levels, so they were given information they had never seen before. It gave them much more responsibility and they could learn by calling in more specialist technical help if they needed it. Workers were given production targets and could take their own decisions, like sending people out for training. In this way, they were managing their own work and that created a very different experience of work.

How do you look back on that time?

It was marvellous! It was a chance to have a hands-on experience of some of the things we were thinking about in the university. One of the reasons I am relatively positive about this idea of 'cells' is that I have seen it happen. That doesn't mean it will work equally well in all circumstances, but I have been a witness to that type of experience.

GOD IS UNTAMEABLE

Your social thinking is inspired by Christianity, but who is God to you?

God is beyond. It's important not to tame God down to my size, to the image that I can have. I always try to remember that God is so much bigger. That tension is important. We can't begin to understand God because our knowledge is so very limited. God is a constantly developing living relationship and we don't know exactly where this relationship is going.

11
Katarina Pajchel

OSLO; INTERVIEW IN ROME

One world, one knowledge

A young Dominican sister and a physicist – an unusual combination? It's a question Katarina Pajchel is often asked. She is currently working in a research group at Oslo University involved in experiments at CERN, the prestigious European organization for nuclear research based just outside Geneva. Katarina is one of more than 3,000 scientists from all over the world working on ATLAS, a particle physics experiment at the Large Hadron Collider.

She began life in a big house in Warsaw, Poland, where three generations lived under one roof. As a child, she enjoyed watching her grandmother, a geologist, working in the garden. Moving to Norway wasn't that bad for little Katarina, who had a problem-free time at a Catholic school in Bergen. Her parents, however, were quite challenged later on when their daughter told them she wanted to be a sister. 'It is an obstacle that a lot of youngsters experience nowadays,' she says. 'The religious life is not accepted easily.'

Nonetheless, Katarina became a sister in her mid-20s and went to live in the Dominican convent Katarinahjemmet in Oslo. When she shows me pictures of the building on her computer, I suddenly recognize the place and remember I stayed there a few years ago when I interviewed two prominent Norwegians: the then Prime Minister Kjelle Bondevik and his Deputy Foreign Minister Janne Haaland Matlary who, as a member of the Pontifical Council for Justice and Peace, recently spoke at the Vatican about the 'enormous female talent of the Church, which should be used more'.

And that is precisely what Katarina Pajchel is doing. She is making use of her talents as a physicist thanks to St Dominic's vision of putting study at the core of his Order. Combining study and prayer, Katarina's life is an answer to those who question her about the two fields she is involved in. 'It's one world – science and theology. I find that working with physics is very often as contemplative as praying in church.'

Katarina Pajchel was born in 1974 in Warsaw and moved to Norway when she was 9. She studied physics in Bergen and Krakow and became a sister at 25. She is living in the convent of the Dominican Sisters of Notre Dame de Grâce in Oslo, also known as Katarinahjemmet. She is currently involved in a scientific research project at CERN in Geneva.

TIME TRAVEL

You are working on the ATLAS experiment at the Large Hadron Collider. Can you tell us the goal of these experiments? Which team are you part of?

I am a member of an experimental particle physics research group at the University of Oslo, which is one of about 180 institutes collaborating in the ATLAS experiment. It is one of the new generation of experiments at CERN. Their main purpose is to learn more about the fundamental building blocks of nature.

We know much about the light particles that make up all we see around us, but by smashing particles at great speed, we accumulate enough energy to create new and heavier particles, in accordance with Einstein's equation which says that energy and mass are closely related. These heavy particles live only a tiny fraction of a second before they decay. So although they may be new in our experiments, they existed naturally when the universe was only fractions of a second old and very hot and dense. In particle collisions at very high energies, we recreate the conditions of the early universe. One can almost think of it as time travel back to the origins. So ultimately, we want to learn more about not only matter, but also the universe and its evolution.

How do I picture you in your daily work? What do you do, specifically?

My work is sort of divided. I work a lot in computing to analyse data and obtain results. Because we are searching for very rare processes, we need to collect enormous amounts of data if we are to have a chance of seeing at least a few of the interesting ones. We are searching for the proverbial needle in the haystack. In order to analyse all this data, we use a worldwide computing network called the Grid. There are more than 3,000 physicists collaborating in these experiments, and by using this tool we can share the data as well as distribute the work in a pool of shared computing resources.

What are you doing with all these data?

Well, that is the other part, the fun part. We analyse them, search for interesting collisions and try to understand the physics behind them. Although we have a theory which describes beautifully our current observations – the so-called Standard Model of particle physics – there are clear indications that this cannot be the full picture. One of the main goals of the experiments is to pin down the nature of the mechanism responsible for the mass of particles – the Higgs mechanism – and to search for new particles. Such new particles and phenomena will give us insight into broader and more fundamental laws of physics.

So, the experiments aim to find an extended theory of the fundamental particles and interactions. Has the research produced any results yet?

No, not yet. We still need to collect more data and we need time to analyse and interpret them. One of the very interesting candidates for such an extended theory is called 'supersymmetry'. One of its appealing features is that it would help us to understand better what the universe is made of. With our current knowledge we can explain only four per cent of the total mass of the universe, which is mainly the stars, objects we can see.

Together with many colleagues around the globe, I look for events that would indicate something new, something that differs from what we would expect. Of course, there are many other groups looking for other particle signatures, and who knows what we will discover?

A SCIENTIST AND A NUN

What led you to become a Dominican sister?

It is the combination of being able to study, pray and preach that makes the Dominican Order unique. In dialogue with my community, we saw that there was indeed space and understanding for this combination so that my work could also include physics. I was touched by one of the Dominican mottos: *Contemplare et contemplate aliis tradere*, meaning 'Contemplate and hand on the fruits of your contemplation'. The dynamics of passing on what you have learned caught me. St Thomas Aquinas is very inspiring in this respect, especially his understanding of study, contemplation and prayer, and what brings them together. In all, he sees a deep search for truth and ultimately God, whether we dive into nature or scripture.

I am also fascinated (a romantic trait of mine perhaps) by mediaeval thought before knowledge branched out into many specializations. In the thirteenth century, Thomas Aquinas and Albert the Great were great scholars and universal thinkers. Albertus Magnus' interests ranged all the way from natural sciences to theology. He is a very interesting figure because of how he combined what later became two separate domains of knowledge. This awareness of there only being one truth has got lost today, although some present-day physicists, like John Polkinghorne, the 2002 Cambridge Templeton Prize winner, subscribes to the view that there is one world and one knowledge of this world. Hence, science and theology cannot be in conflict in their search for truth.

Who has been an inspiration on your journey?

I am inspired by Simon Tugwell, who has written extensively about Dominican spirituality and the early Dominicans in particular. When I read his book *The Way of the Preacher*, I thought, 'This is how I want to live!' As a witness. Tugwell describes the driving force of the friars in our Order at the beginning. Another aspect I was touched by was his emphasis on dialogue. As Dominicans, we pass on the things we have learned, not as teachers from above or by giving ready-made answers, but by accompanying people and being honest. Even when we are walking in the desert and seeking faith, we are still serving others as we all share the same questions in our secularized Western society, which is suffering from spiritual poverty. Faith, meaning and sense of life are pivotal questions.

Another significant writer for me is Simone Weil, a French philosopher who died in the mid-twentieth century. In her book *Waiting for God*, she wrote about the right use of study and its relationship to prayer. She pointed out how study, understood as attention, is a preparation for prayer. This contemplative dimension of study and the waiting to receive knowledge from God is also a preparation for meeting the other person.

How did your parents react to your decision to become a Dominican sister?

To be honest, they were not too happy with it. But I'm afraid this may be an experience I share with many people who choose religious life nowadays.

What arguments did you use to defend your decision?

I'm not sure there were many arguments. At a certain point, you just have to live this life and hope that it becomes an argument in itself.

Isn't it strange for a religious person to be involved in physics?

Why should it be strange? I believe science and theology point towards one and the same reality, although from very different angles.

But I admit that, statistically speaking, religious people are more often to be found studying theology, philosophy and social sciences or involved in social work and education. Nor should one underestimate the impact of the myth that there is a war between faith and science. But it is very much a myth, because history proves that many religious people have been involved in science. What also makes the picture more complex are the controversies in the United States between creationists and the advocates of intelligent design, and the stronger atheistic voices represented by people like Richard Dawkins.

So, it is true that many people experience a split between modern technological and scientific culture and spiritual life; but for me they belong together; they need not fear each other. Christianity has deep philosophical roots; there is room for rationality. Rationality and faith are not opposites!

How do you preach?

I see my research as my preaching. It is evident that you can be part of today's scientific culture and still be a religious person. You don't have to turn off your brain as a believer. By giving lectures and presentations, I try to show that there are religious people working in technological fields who are not alienated from present-day society. I also hope that being a believer in a university milieu can be an important sign.

Is it difficult to be a Christian at university?

I personally don't experience that in Norway. In my group at the University of Oslo, people know by now that I am a sister, and although they may not agree with the Catholic Church, they show me a lot of respect.

When the film *Angels and Demons*, based on the novel by Dan Brown, was screened, our university group was asked to give a presentation about fact and fiction in the film. I was very much surprised to be asked explicitly to say something about the religious dimension of the film. In my lecture, I had prepared a small personal part in which I pointed out that we physicists are not only materialists. Not everybody in our group may be interested in religion, but many engage in philosophical reflections, despite the common view of physicists as nerds. So we struggle with this nerdy image, but we consider our work to be deeply ingrained in our culture.

CREATIONISM

What's your opinion about creationism and intelligent design?

They are two different things. I definitely don't agree with creationism, because it comes down to a literal way of reading the scripture, which I think is wrong. In Scandinavia, we have a strong Protestant biblical tradition, and many people think Christians read the Bible literally. But I believe the Bible was not intended to be read like a science book. Nevertheless, I am also very sceptical of the intelligent design models, because they tend to introduce the 'God of gaps' concept where 'God' is used to fill the holes in our scientific knowledge. This kind of interpretation does an injustice to both religion and the natural sciences.

Who is God to you?

The image of the Creator, the life-giver, is important for me. The Creator often emerges in the psalms, which form my daily prayer. I also see God as the one who loves us and wants our lives to become full; the one who calls us and gives meaning and direction to our lives. This act of loving creation, of calling to life, is in a way echoed in the mission of Christ, who overcomes sin and death.

THE WHITE HABIT

Do you go to the university dressed in your white habit? Can you choose when or where to wear it?

We do indeed have this sort of basic freedom. When deciding whether or not to wear the habit in a given community and milieu, you need some delicacy and understanding of when it's more practical or appropriate. Personally, I use it at least part of the day, usually for Lauds and Mass in the morning.

When I go to university, I don't wear the habit because I want to interact with my colleagues as a physicist, and so I follow the informal academic dress code. When my colleagues learned that I was a sister, they didn't have any problems with that. And we have some funny practical things in common: while my colleagues have to run to get their children on time from kindergarten, I have to run to be in time for vespers.

We find it important to wear the habit when we do something as a community or in church, like participating in meetings, youth gatherings or giving a lecture. In those instances, it illustrates that we represent something more than ourselves and we want to be visible as such to the outside world.

Have you ever had any negative reactions towards your wearing a habit on the streets?

No, not really. Surprisingly, negative reactions tend to come more from Catholics who have stereotypes of what a sister is. But I did experience something interesting just recently. I went for a Sunday walk with a friend, and some 13-year-old boys came toward us on their skateboards – you know, the type with their trousers hanging round their knees. They looked at me in my white habit and asked, 'Are you a nun?' When I said yes, they said, 'Cool. I didn't know there were nuns in Norway. Cool!' So you never know what reactions will come your way.

Do you perceive a tension between traditional and progressive sisters in general? Is wearing a habit seen as traditional?

It is a complex issue, but it seems that there may be a trend, at least in Europe, where some young sisters are more interested in going back to the roots and to what they see as traditional.

We recently had a meeting of young Dominican sisters in Europe and as we shared our experiences, it became clear that both in western and central Europe, there is a longing for religious life to be seen as truly alternative and radically visible. I admit this could be perceived as superficial – that's where the habit comes in – but there is definitely a search for authenticity, credibility and the right kind of authority.

Sometimes it looks as if some younger sisters get along better with sisters of two generations older than they do with sisters of their parents' generation. But that is a general trend perceived in society as a whole, and religious life is no exception to that. It makes sense if you look at it as the pendulum swinging to and fro. We have been brought up to question everything, and we are thankful to the previous generation for that, but we also need answers, we need people we can trust. It doesn't mean that we want to accept everything. No; we want dialogue. And that's where our Dominican way of preaching can meet the needs of a secularized world marked by spiritual poverty and an often fumbling search for meaning.

How do you look upon this blind quest for meaning?

People may be hesitant to use the word 'faith', but surely they are looking for direction and some broader perspectives on life. Although sensational and superficial thriller novels about Christianity sell like hot cakes, we shouldn't condemn the interest in them. This sometimes chaotic and confused search and critical questioning is our ally, not our enemy. It is the soil in which we can sow our seeds. We could be instruments to make the word of God resonate in this society that is full of questions about the meaning of life.

12
Emilio Platti

Learning from what is strange

Emilio Platti is enthusiastic. Together with Jean-Jacques Pérennès, he is promoting his new book, *Islam: Friend or Foe*, at the Islamic University in Jakarta and taking part in debates. Platti is pleasantly surprised by the openness that he finds at this Indonesian university. Tomorrow, they will travel to other university cities to engage in similar debates.

Emilio's parents may have destined him for a multicultural life. His Flemish mother fell in love with a handsome Italian immigrant. They were the talk of the town when they got married in the 30s. Little Emilio heard Dutch, Italian and French at home, but nothing predetermined him to study Arabic! Emilio was only 16 when his father died. At 19 he decided to become a Dominican because he loved studying. Why did he one day write in fine handwriting the first Sura of the Koran, the Fâtiha? And why, two years later, did he ask for permission to read the Koran, which was still on the list of prohibited books at that time?

He started visiting the poorer districts in Brussels, where the immigrants were welcomed in the Foyer des Jeunes and the Centre El-Kalima. The world opened up even more when Emilio received a scholarship that set him on the road to Cairo, where he met Father Georges Anawati, a respected Dominican theologian and Islamic professor, who introduced him to the Christian Arab medieval literature of Baghdad. Platti became a highly esteemed professor in Islamic studies and now commutes between Leuven and the Dominican Centre in Cairo.

He speaks passionately to me about his involvement in the dialogues between Christianity and Islam and between Islam

135

and modernity. Yet, he is not blind to the growth of a militant form of Islam which threatens Christians and Muslims alike. In response to this rising fundamentalism, the Cairo Dominicans have built the world's best library on Arabic religious heritage to encourage mutual understanding. I wonder whether dialogue will prevail over violence.

> Emilio Platti was born in 1943 in Ronse, Belgium of Italian-Flemish parents. He is a member of the Dominican Institute of Oriental Studies (IDEO) in Cairo, a professor emeritus of Islamic theology at the Catholic University of Leuven, Belgium and the Catholic Institute of Paris, France. In the 2008 Forum for Interreligious Dialogue in Rome (a joint initiative of Pope Benedict XVI and Prince Ghazi bin Muhammad bin Talal of Jordan), he participated as an expert on Islam-Christian exchange.

PRAYER AND VIOLENCE

With the terrorist attacks of recent years, suspicion of Islam has grown. Are those feelings justified?

When one is in a mosque, as we are now, such feelings are not justified. This is a place of serenity. People who are praying address God and turn towards the *mihrab*, the prayer niche. The primary meaning of Islam is 'piety'. Muslims see themselves not as absolute beings with unlimited freedom, but as dependent on others and, above all on God. The call '*Allahu Akbar*', 'God is greater than I', expresses this.

Then how do you explain the fear of Islam felt by the man in the street?

With the political twists of the last 25 years, political Islam, Wahhabism, the Taliban and Al Qaeda have totally distorted the image of Islam. The essential meaning of this religion escapes many. On top of this, most Westerners are no longer sensitive to the faith dimension of life, while Muslims still are.

And yet, Muslims are sometimes incited to violence during prayer. How does that square with the faith dimension?

That is a deviation that we have also known in Christianity – remember the crusades. Moreover, the Koran is extremely sensitive about injustice, and the whole being of the believer is involved in prayer. On the one hand, that can derail, but on the other hand, it can also create commitment to justice. There have been times when Christianity has been devotional but completely neglected commitment.

WHY DO THEY HATE US?

After the attacks in New York, many wonder where the Muslims' hatred of the West comes from. What is your answer?

There are two important elements: modernity and the historical aspect. The French Muslim Abdelwahab Meddeb has written a book entitled *La maladie de l'Islam* – the sickness of Islam. After periods of greatness – look at Istanbul, Cairo, Baghdad – the Muslim world has stopped to wonder. 'Where are we now? We used to be the greatest civilization!' Around the sixteenth and seventeenth centuries, the West developed extraordinary dynamism in the form of journeys of discovery, technological developments and trade relations, while the economy of the Islamic world declined. According to Meddeb, there has been a growing resentment in the Islamic community that has in some groups turned into aggression. They believe that the West must have done this to them. Others seek the reason for this in themselves.

Do some Muslims blame the West for the fact that they have failed to enter modernity?

It is more complex than that. There is just as much real fascination and admiration for the achievements of the West. So it's not just jealousy. It's a double feeling. Some Muslim intellectuals want to break out of the rigidity: 'Must we take everything in the Koran literally?' In Egypt, for example, the punishment for theft – cutting off a hand – is no longer applied. They have understood that this is a poor application of a medieval rule of law from the Koran. If you want to be a good Muslim, you must seek a punishment that is morally sounder than the old one.

Tariq Ramadan, a Swiss scholar of Islam, says that the Muslims' great sickness comes from systematically laying the blame at the door of others and seeing themselves as victims. What do you think?

On the one hand, it is naturally easy to seek to blame the West for your own failings, on the other hand, there really have been abuses. Colonial France, for instance, claimed to be bringing civilization to north Africa. The Egyptian theologian Mohammed Abduh notes that the French simply wished to impose their ascendancy in trade. He says, 'I have read the Bible, and I admire the wonderful figure of Jesus Christ, but I don't recognize him anywhere in your colonial civilization.'

JIHAD

What does jihad mean? It is most often translated as 'holy war'!

That is incorrect. The term is loaded in various ways, but the most correct meaning is 'exerted effort'. Although *jihad* can be used in association with another concept in the Koran, namely *qitaal*, armed struggle. But *jihad* also means striving for humanity by, for example, showing respect for your parents, even when they are old, or by being fair with people you do business with, or by caring for the poor and for orphans. These are fundamental precepts.

Is that jihad?

It is indeed. It is a moral effort that makes you more human.

Don't you think that the average Muslim understands jihad to mean 'armed struggle'?

The average Muslim would immediately understand what I'm saying. There is great ambiguity in our society. The expansion of Islam has indeed proceeded through violence; but the British didn't expand their empire peacefully, and neither did any of the other Western peoples!

Christians like to point to Jesus and His peacefulness, but forget that Christian piety was certainly not always put into practice. And they look down on Islam from this Christian sensitivity and say, 'Islam doesn't have that.' No, Islam doesn't have that. Islam orders society in accordance with laws and rules of behaviour. The Koran clearly states that weapons may be used as a means of defence in situations of injustice. Do the Muslims have sufficient reason to feel that they have been treated unjustly? Well, many experience the situation in Palestine as deeply unjust. Let me point out that the West used weapons in Kosovo to end the conflict.

Muslim students ask me, 'Is Christendom not hypocritical? After all, America, a country that calls itself Christian, uses weapons too!' Do you see the double standards in our criticism of Islam and *jihad*? It goes without saying that the conflict in Palestine does not warrant the extreme terrorist reactions we saw in New York.

Why do so few Muslims condemn those terrorist attacks?

On the one hand, the media give a one-sided picture. When a mosque in Karachi was bombed, the Great Imam of Cairo strongly condemned the attack, but that wasn't front-page news. On the other hand, the average Muslim is specifically challenged to ponder on his identity and clearly state his views on terrorism.

We see that places where Islam comes in contact with Christianity often become powder kegs. Why is that?

Let us not forget that, as we see in the Koran and with Muhammad, there is a strong and natural liking for Jesus and Christians. Islam arose in reaction not to Christianity, but to the polytheism of Mecca! But over the course of history, the Koran discovered certain pronouncements about Jesus and the Trinity, found them strange and rejected them. A while later, the Arabian armies came into conflict with the Byzantines, and so the expansion proceeded. That conflict between Islam and Christianity has weighed heavily in the past. Think of the Reconquista, when the Iberian peninsula was taken back from the Moors, or the Balkan wars.

Do the Muslims recognize a central authority?

In that respect, you cannot compare the Islamic world with the Catholic Church. There is no pope and no hierarchy of bishops. But there are people who hold authority. They are chiefly lawyers appointed to certain functions by the authorities in Islamic countries and can issue authoritative *fatwas* or recommendations. There are also specialists in Islamic law, the Koran, the Sunnah, the life of the Prophet. These people act as a point of reference in case there are problems. The best known is naturally the Ayatollah Khomeini, who in 1990 pronounced the *fatwa* against the author Salman Rushdie on account of his descriptions of Muhammad in his novel *The Satanic Verses*.

The big problem is that Islam has been identified with the foundations of a state for the past 12 centuries. The whole body of legislation is built on the principles of the Koran and the teachings of Muhammad. A couple of hundred years ago, the construction began to crumble under the influence of Western colonialism, leaving the Islamic world in search of its identity as a consequence. Some want to reintroduce *sharia* law. *Sharia* actually means the 'divine' law that Muslim lawyers laid down in a legal system called the *Fiqh*. But society evolves, and going back in time never works.

LETTER VERSUS SPIRIT

What are the greatest similarities between Christianity and Islam?

The Ten Commandments appear in the Torah of the Jews, the Christian Bible and the Koran of the Muslims. There is a shared feeling for justice; respect for others; care for orphans, widows, the poor; and the pious person's relationship with God. Dialogue must therefore go back to the deepest core of religious identity. The sticking points in the dialogue remain the historical events. The most studied books in our library concern the crusades.

And the differences between the two religions?

In Christianity, the focus is on the relationship between God,

Jesus and humanity. At Christmas, we hear that 'God's grace appeared among men in Jesus Christ.' Islam, by contrast, focuses on the Koran. God's law, to which man must submit, is compulsory. That is an important difference in emphasis with Christianity. And yet the forerunner of both religions is Judaism, where the emphasis is on the law. That detailed legislation does not appear in the New Testament, however, because Jesus spiritualized the law. That is a radical innovation in Christianity, compared with Judaism and Islam.

What do you mean by 'spiritualization' of the law?

The New Testament recounts the life of Jesus. But Jesus handed down no specific laws and rules. He rebuked the Pharisees for their obsession with applying the rules while neglecting the deeper dimensions of belief. We find the same approach in Paul. As a Jew, he understood the legal aspect of Judaism and the Torah very well. The core of his preaching concerned the Christian's freedom from the letter of the law.

The Koran pays much more attention to moral life and rules of behaviour. In Christianity, the sacraments are signs of God's love. By contrast, Islam is built up as a legal system that supports the organization of a state.

Hence the entanglement of religion and state in Islam.

Indeed. The state is responsible for the ethical character of society, and must lay down laws. This is how society becomes human, according to Muslims. And this is where we see a great difference between Islam and Christianity where there has been a division between Church and State for centuries.

How has Christianity managed to adapt to modern society while Islam finds that difficult?

Some scholars – although there is no unanimity on the matter – believe that the Islamic legal system has fossilized. If you hold on to the laws so tightly, no evolution is possible. In our parliaments, new laws are passed every day, adapting to a changing society. In the Islamic world, that adaptation hasn't happened.

When did that process of fossilization begin?

Very early – perhaps already in the eleventh or twelfth century. But to begin with, no one noticed. It wasn't until the seventeenth and eighteenth centuries that people started to speak of the current crisis in the Islamic world. Because Islam sees itself as a global structure, it has fallen into crisis in relation to the West, not only in relation to Christianity.

Can Islam be integrated in the West?

That depends on how the Muslim world manages to detach itself from this global legal identity that strives for dominance. If Islam can reinvent its identity from its deepest religious and mystical core, then it will be able to integrate in the West.

NOT ON THE CROSS

Can Muslims understand the crucifixion of Christ?

With great difficulty. The Koran is ambiguous about the cross as the Christian path to God. Muslims disapprove of the cross because it has become a political symbol that is branded in their collective memory. The problem is that, historically, the cross has two meanings. On the one hand, it is the victory of Constantine and the crusaders, on the other, it is Christ's humiliating death. But the second meaning doesn't occur in the Koran, because it is absolutely unthinkable in Islam that an authentic prophet like Jesus could be crucified.

Wasn't Jesus a prophet, then, according to Islam?

Quite the contrary – He was indeed a prophet, and one of the greatest!

How does the Koran deal with that contradiction?

The Koran is ambiguous in this respect. Before Jesus was crucified, God took Him into Heaven. So the Holy Week is simply deleted and the Koran skips ahead to the Ascension. The whole subject of Holy Week, the crucifixion and resurrection disappears. Just as God helped Muhammad to victory on his first battlefield, so God exalted Jesus immediately and He is one of the greatest saints and prophets in history. But He is not the son of God because, according to the Koran, God has no son.

Which other elements of Christianity are rejected?

The unique relationship of Jesus to the Father, the Trinity, man's salvation through Christ. In that way, you remove the concept of redemption and the very heart of Christianity. But Islam has no problem with the figure of Mary as the virgin mother of Jesus who was born without sin.

MUTTON WITH FRIES

Were there ever problems with Islam in the Foyer des Jeunes, the youth centre for young Moroccans in Brussels?

Never. I remember in the early years of the Foyer, during the sacrificial feast, a sheep would be slaughtered and everybody would eat mutton with fries! In those days, Islam was a religion that nobody had problems with. It wasn't until the assassination of the Egyptian President Anwar Sadat in 1981 that a militant branch of Islam came into the picture. The Iranian revolution also played a role. That movement wanted to win an identity and accused the western European powers of having colonized the Muslim countries in a purely materialistic way for the last 200 years. When the movement saw that it couldn't gain power, it resorted to terrorism. Egypt suffered heavy terrorist attacks from 1981 to 1997. Algeria went the same way.

How has this anti-Western movement spread?

Wahhabism, the ideology of Saudi Arabia, has spread through the oil dollars of the Al Saud family. The movement, which started at the end of the eighteenth century, seeks identity in a uniform Islam that is both rigorous and anti-Sufi. It is of course also anti-Western, but because at the same time petroleum agreements were signed with the West, that aspect has never fully come to light and the role of Saudi Arabia has been greatly downplayed. Osama Bin Laden had some of his roots in this ideology. This form of Islam is also promoted in many mosques and centres of study.

One of my students, who is writing a thesis on Wahhabist influences in Nigeria, has established that the great brotherhoods that used to be anchored in African Islam are being boycotted in favour of this strict version of Islam. The same thing is happening in Indonesia, where moderate Muslims are complaining about the spread of Wahhabism through the internet and in schools.

What is the influence of this political, or 'identitary' version of Islam?

The popular devotion and the spiritual aspect of Islam are coming under fire. Fundamentalists are not shying away from blowing up popular holy places, as has happened in Pakistan. So there is a crisis within the Muslim community itself, and the answer must also be found there. But it is easy to underestimate the pressure of collective censure in a working-class neighbourhood. Moreover, the spiritual aspect of Islam present in Sufism is repressed in favour of the legalistic character of political Islam that seeks to impose a particular lifestyle, such as segregating men and women.

CHRISTIANS IN MUSLIM AREAS

What are the consequences for Christians in Muslim areas?

At present, there are two identitary movements. The nationalist identitary movement emphasizes nationalism. In Palestine, you can be Christian or Muslim, provided you are primarily Palestinian. The Islamic identitary movement, by contrast, tolerates no forms other than the so-called pure Islam, and then, of course, Christians are targeted.

How do you see this developing?

Badly in the case of Palestine and Iraq, where Christians are persecuted. I have underestimated the role of Wahhabism in Saudi Arabia because that movement is financially so strong. We have had to abandon our priory in Mosul to seek safety in

Kurdistan. If Wahhabism spreads further in Egypt, the Copts will face the same problem. Until now, Egyptian or Arab nationalism has won out, so there is no problem, since Copts are also Egyptians.

Do Muslims practise polygamy?

Yes, but in Egypt, at least, it is not common. You should know that 20 per cent of the 85 million Egyptians have to live on less than one euro a day. None of those 20 per cent can afford to keep two wives. The rich can, of course – officially, it is permitted to have up to four wives. But Muslims say that the West is hypocritical, because there are many more extramarital relationships in the West than there are in Islam, where relationships are at least regularized.

Would a woman caught in adultery be stoned in Egypt?

No! Do you know what happens? Her husband sends her away, has the fact officially registered and then marries someone else. The rejected woman can then marry her lover.

And sharia?

It is not so strictly applied as in Saudi Arabia or Iran, but we only hear about those cases, of course. You shouldn't forget that social control is extremely powerful. It is not done to stand kissing in the street!

FOREIGNER

Why did you become a Dominican?

It was a rational step. I didn't know the Dominicans personally. I was looking for an order that was both monastic and intellectual. The Dominicans' choral prayer, intellectual leanings and openness to the world appealed to me. You could laconically say that as a Dominican you enter the priory in order to leave it again as quickly as possible! We are preachers, and we roam around. Back in the thirteenth and fourteenth centuries, right after the Order was founded, Dominic sent his brothers out into the world.

Many left in the 1960s. Why did you stay?

Because I have found my path. My commitment to the Foyer in Brussels was very important, together with the intellectual challenges I was seeking in the 60s. That was the time of Edward Schillebeeckx, the great Flemish theologian, who emigrated to the Netherlands. Georges Anawati also played a role for me: he was one of the founders of IDEO, and an Egyptian Dominican and Islamologist.

Have you ever considered becoming a Muslim?

One of my friends became a Muslim. He asked me to convert, too, but I can't. Christianity points me to Christ, and awakens me to God.

Who is God for you?

He is the one who has carried and structured my life because I have now truly become an apostle of Christianity. The Gospel, the figure of Christ, has helped me to develop that openness to people, especially foreigners. My mother, too, played an important role. My father died when I was 16. When I was 19, I joined the Dominicans, which was not an easy step because it meant my mother could no longer carry on my father's business. But she respected what drove me. I am very grateful to my parents, who were both deeply Catholic.

Now you are a foreigner again, this time in Cairo. Have you ever been threatened?

I once had a knife at my gut in a crowded bus in Cairo. Someone shouted, 'There are thieves on the bus!' I happened to be standing at the open door, and a man came towards me with a knife drawn and called, 'Let me out!' The people pulled me back to free the exit for him. I shall never forget those passengers' concern for me. What was funny was that, just as the thief was about to jump out of the bus, one of the passengers called out to him, 'Look out! Don't jump now – there's a car coming!' I found that so human, so typically Egyptian. My being a foreigner has never been a barrier. And conversely, I myself have always been fascinated by the other. The strange is something to learn from.

13

Dominika and Natallia

BELARUS

The dream of a new foundation

Sisters Natallia and Dominika are young nuns who were born in Belarus and carried out their novitiate in Poland and, in secret, in Lithuania. They are living in a contemplative monastery in Europe at present and hope to establish the first foundation of contemplative nuns in Belarus in the future. Only their first names are used in this interview in the interests of their safety.

A FEARFUL SILENCE

When did you realize that the world was not as good a place as you had expected as children?

Dominika: When I was about 9 years old, I went to church and saw a lot of people crying at the door because the priest had been taken away for interrogation. They were all afraid he was going to be imprisoned in Siberia. When I asked my parents about it, they kept a fearful silence. It was not to be discussed!

Natallia: During the Communist persecution, our Catholic church was turned into a factory, while the Orthodox church and the synagogue were converted into storage depots. After *perestroika* (the democratization movement in the former Soviet Union), the Catholic and Orthodox churches were restored but the synagogue has disappeared.

Sister Dominika, why did you want to become a Dominican nun?

At first, I didn't know what a 'nun' was! There were no contemplative monasteries in Belarus, so I had no idea what a religious

life could entail. But one day, when I was in church with my
mother, a young woman asked me in a whisper if I wanted to
come 'for adoration'. I had never heard the word before, but
my mother nodded. This woman was apparently a Dominican
sister, but she didn't wear a habit, as that was forbidden. Sister
Agnes, as she was called, led me to a special room where the
Blessed Sacrament was exposed. When I asked her what I had
to do, she answered: 'Nothing, you only have to be!' I thought
that would be easy!

Later, when I was 15, Sister Agnes invited me to visit her in
Minsk to meet the other sisters. After a year, she asked me if I
wanted to give my life to God as a nun. I was surprised because
there was no monastery in Belarus, but she explained, 'It is
possible: you'll found the first one!' I joined the Dominicans
because they were the only nuns present at the time.

How did your parents react?

I didn't say anything for a long time, because Sister Agnes
warned me it could be dangerous if the Communists found
out. In Vilnius in Lithuania, where the nuns came together
every weekend in a small house, the Blessed Sacrament had
to be hidden. When I wanted to start novitiate, I wasn't
allowed to without my parents' consent. When I finally told
my mum, she said, 'I know. I was waiting for you to tell me.
But it is not my decision – it is between you and God.' It
was more difficult for my father because he was disabled –
both his hands were paralysed. I was his favourite child and
I had been taking care of him for years; washing, dressing
and feeding him. I couldn't bring myself to tell him, so I
asked my mother to. As he was a very religious person, he
accepted my decision. However, he told me he thought I
would change my mind because I was so young, adding that
he would always welcome me back. I was heartbroken when
I had to leave him.

I started novitiate at 18. After receiving the habit, I had to
hide it in a closet and continue my life with my family for
two years, so as not to raise suspicion. Only on Saturdays and
Sundays could I go to Minsk to pray with the other nuns. Once
a month, we went to Vilnius, where about 16 nuns were living

in houses spread throughout the village. They didn't wear their habits because everything had to be done in secret.

TO BE CLOSE TO GOD

Did you have a boyfriend at school?

I had a few. Nobody knew who I really was and if you had a boyfriend, you didn't raise suspicion! But I never seriously loved anybody because God took my heart from a very early age. Before any boy came along, God opened my heart for Him. To be close to God was something I longed for! I can't explain how it happened; it was not over night. I'm only starting to realize what it means to be a Dominican nun. When sister Agnes took me for adoration when I was a child, she meant me to be in the presence of God. I now realize that my vocation is to be.

Have your parents visited you here?

No. My father has already died and it is difficult for my mother to get a visa, but I am allowed to visit her once every two years.

Sister Natallia, why did you want to be a Dominican nun?

When I was about 17, I didn't believe in God. I often gave my parents a hard time. Nothing could reach me, because we were always told at school that God didn't exist and I believed it.

Once, after a quarrel with my parents, I sneaked to church where some seminarians told us about their vocation. Suddenly, my heart was touched because I felt that if these young seminarians had given their lives to God, it was something very truthful, no matter what I had been told at school. When I realized that death is not the end, as my teachers so often insisted, I was flooded with happiness. The odd thing is that I started to pray for all the people who didn't believe. My desire was to get married and have a big family so that I could tell my children about this God I had discovered. It was a long time before I realized that God was gently inviting me to lead my life differently.

When I finally entered the monastery, I was surprised to hear that St Dominic had prayed in a similar way: 'Lord, what will happen to sinners?' I had experienced the same pain in my heart for others. So, basically, I wanted to become a nun to pray for the salvation of souls.

What kind of persecution could you face during Communism?

At school, they taught atheism. It was forbidden to speak about God, unless it was to scoff at religion. You had to wear a kind of 'Lenin badge'. If you were suspected of having religious inclinations, the badge was taken away and you were bullied. When I was 8, my mum gave me a necklace with a little miraculous medal, but I couldn't wear it at school. No crosses, no Bibles, no holy pictures – nothing was tolerated in public! During Stalin's regime, crosses would be removed from private homes and you could be sent to prison or carried off to Siberia for having one. Nevertheless, there were religious communities in hiding. Nowadays, the situation is improving slowly. According to our constitutions, we need only nine nuns to make a foundation. But we are not yet ready for a possible foundation in Belarus. We need to grow more in contemplative life.

PRESENCE

Do you ever doubt your faith?

Dominika: Not especially, but I have many questions. When our community in Minsk closed down, I realized that, for the time being, a monastery in Belarus was not possible, and this was very painful for me. Most difficult, though, is that I am living here while I often think about a foundation in Belarus. Sometimes, it is as if there are two poles in my mind that are difficult to connect.

What is the best thing about living here?

Dominika: I never imagined that it could be possible to accept one another completely. I thought it was only possible in Heaven, but I found true acceptance in this monastery. Another thing that is bringing me great joy is the daily silent Eucharistic adoration.

Natallia: To be together with different nationalities; the silence and respect for one another is something I value enormously.

What does the exposition of the Blessed Sacrament mean to you? What do you feel in adoration?

Dominika: I can think of only one word, 'presence!' It may sound strange, but I don't feel anything really. I am reminded of what Sister Agnes told me as a child: 'You don't have to do anything, you only have to be.' Each nun is assigned a specific time for adoration, approximately two hours each day. Sometimes it is difficult and I get bored, but on the whole I like it very much because I like just being with God.

Natallia: Getting bored is something normal, I think. I try to avoid it by paying special attention to my thoughts when I feel weariness setting in.

How do you live the rhythm of daily prayer? Wouldn't it be better to hold the prayer services one after the other and so be free for the rest of the day?

Dominika: That would be like eating all your meals together, breakfast, dinner, supper, and then being free for the rest of the day!

How do you get into contemplation? How do you pray?

Natallia: Contemplation is pure grace from God; you can't produce it. Reading the scriptures, praying in Mass, going to the garden, seeing flowers – everything can lead me into contemplation.

Dominika: We sometimes dance during recreation. Our former Prioress is very good at folk dancing. Praying is like dancing because it takes two to dance; you can't dance alone. God and I, we are together. Sometimes, I pray silently in meditation, while, at other times, I need words to lead me into silence.

Part of your prayer is interceding for others. Isn't that telling God what He has to do?

Natallia: A few years ago, when I was in Krakow, Sister Stephania was very ill. During the night I got up to look after her, and when I went back to my room I was worried and didn't know what to do. Finally I said, 'Lord, she is suffering. You are like a mother and a father; she is your child. I ask grace for her, not for me.' This is my life, my vocation: to intercede for others. It is not what we want, but what God wants.

The Dominicans are associated with the rosary. What about the endless repetitions of words? Doesn't it become empty?

Dominika: When I was a child and my grandmother put me to bed, she prayed the rosary when she thought I had fallen asleep. But I was only pretending to be asleep because I was fascinated by what she was doing. One day I took her rosary away from her and put it into my pocket because I wanted to ask her about it, but I forgot. It was a little embarrassing for me to explain why I had done it, but she gently explained to me it was about 'praying'. So, the rosary has always been a part of my life.

I don't see it as an empty repetition of words. If you love somebody, you also keep repeating the same words of love over and over again. Do lovers ever get tired of that? Saying the rosary is like being with your Mother continually, in the presence of the mysteries of her Son who loved you first and whom you love.

SPEAK TO ME

What words or phrases are precious to you?

Natallia: Jesus tells Catherine, 'Think of me and I will think of you.' When I am with Him in my thoughts, I feel He cares about me. It has been a slow process to realize this and it is always difficult to explain because it runs so deep and is inexpressible.

Dominika: I am touched by the spirituality of St Catherine of Siena, which reminds me of fire. I wrote the final paper for my theology diploma about her writings on self-knowledge. The more I study her work, the more I love her prayers. I also like the Jesus prayer and the nine ways of praying of St Dominic. When I start painting an icon, I ask the icon to speak to me. Dominic's saying 'He spoke only of and to God' touches me deeply, as does the way he prays for young Dominicans. He doesn't pray in a formal way – his prayer comes from his heart. The expression of Catherine of Siena, 'I am He who is and you are she who is not,' reveals the essence of the truth about me and about God.

What is truth?

The love of God.

You are cloistered. Aren't you fleeing from the world?

Natallia: On the contrary, I am praying for the world, not fleeing from it. We do know what is going on out there. People ask us to pray for healing of an illness, when children are ill, or for drink and drug problems. Living in a monastery, close to God, gives me the opportunity to look on the world with God's eyes and not with my judging eyes.

Dominika: Being in silence gives us the opportunity to see better what people really need. It is like sand clouding water. Water in turmoil becomes turbid, while still water is transparent. In the same way, things become clear in silence. Sometimes people ask us to pray for something specific, but deep problems are hidden underneath. We try to see what they really need.

Christianity is often reproached for putting too much stress on the cross. Can Christians be joyful?

Natallia: After death, there is resurrection. When we unite our suffering with Him, it makes sense.

Dominika: It is not suffering but love that brings about the resurrection! The Paschal mystery can't be separated from the resurrection. The cross is in the middle. When we all pass away and leave this world, we will continue to live forever in love.

Who is God to you? Do you speak to Him?

Natallia: God is everything. He is like my mother and my father, always inviting me and never forcing me. Yes, I speak to Him, during Mass, in singing the psalms. I often simply pray, 'Jesus, I need you, I need you.' I read that some people hear His voice, but I don't hear Him in that way.

Dominika: I always see God in the story of the prodigal son, the father who is waiting. I don't speak to Him as such because my desire can't be expressed in words.

How do you know all this is not an illusion? Perhaps atheists and Communists are right.

Natallia: Nobody can satisfy another person completely, even if you have found your perfect love. Only God can satisfy us completely. As St Augustine said, 'You created us for yourself and we are restless until we rest in you.' I am convinced that I didn't produce this belief myself. I have seen how destructive atheism can be. Atheistic thoughts easily lead to emptiness and they can ruin relationships. In Belarus, abortion is permitted when you have already had two children, so you can kill your foetus whenever you want!

YOU DON'T PREACH!

'Brothers preach and nuns pray.' Isn't that a clear distinction St Dominic made?

Natallia: On the contrary, St Dominic said that the nuns come first in preaching. The brothers put seed in the ground and with our prayers, we tend it so that it grows. He first founded a monastery for the nuns, the brothers came afterwards.

You belong to the Order of Preachers. Yet, you don't preach do you?

Dominika: But look at us: we preach every hour; we never stop! Once, when I was wearing my habit on a 12-hour journey from Poland to Belarus, I met a young man on the train. He reproached me for being in a monastery. He said, 'You are not preaching!' I answered, 'If I started preaching here in the middle of the train, do you think people would believe me? Even my own sister doesn't accept my way of life. But just look at me: my whole life is an act of preaching because of my decision to be a nun.'

When I lived in Belarus, I once got on the bus wearing my habit and funny things happened. Half of the people on the bus approved of my being a nun, the other half didn't. They started arguing among themselves. 'She should get married and have children!' While others answered, 'No, you don't understand. She's doing the right thing!' You see, I preach just by being!

14
Kim En Joong

Painter of the inner light

Booyo, South-Korea, 10 September 1941, the first birthday of little Kim! On a low table, a few objects are displayed: some silver coins, a book, a string of thread. If he reaches for the silver, he'll be rich. Choosing the book could mean that he'll become a lawyer. But the child doesn't glance at any of these objects. Instead he stretches his little hands towards the light of the candle that has been put on the table to illuminate the objects. Light? Is this little boy choosing the light? His parents try again to have him pick one of the objects, but in vain. It is the light that he wants.

'The painter of white', as Timothy Radcliffe has called Kim En Joong, has led quite an extraordinary life. The more I talk to him, the more I am touched by his profound belief and his love of Christ. I first saw his paintings, with their fiery streaks and bright colours, on the walls of the Santa Sabina in Rome. When later I met him in Paris, he explained his fascination for light: 'Light is love. I have always wanted to create a non-polluted world, a world that hints at another life, the life of the mystery.'

Through the years, his exhibitions have proliferated, from Tokyo to San Francisco, but fame hasn't corrupted him. Each time I meet Father Kim, I am greeted by his soft gaze, that contrasts so strongly with the brightness of his palette. Kim has created a powerful composition in red and white glass, leaping like flame towards the ceiling, for a new priory in the Belgian university town of Louvain-la-Neuve. Cardinal Danneels, a good friend of Kim's, blessed the stained glass in the egg-shaped church.

The Iraqi Dominicans, too, dare to build in time of war! They have the bold plan of building an open university for Muslims and Christians in Baghdad, and Father Kim will give colour to a monumental, six-metre-high rose window. I wonder how long it will be before the complex will be bombed to rubble in that war zone. But the Dominicans are adamant: 'If the building is flattened, we'll start again!'

And Father Kim? 'I want to pray a lot and work a lot,' he says. 'And so must you,' he adds in passing. 'I hope that my work contributes to the salvation of the world,' he continues. 'Blessed Dominic wept at night for sinners, while cultivating joy by day.' It is already evening when I leave the Dominican priory, where joy and friendship have been sealed with bread and wine.

Kim En Joong was born in 1940 in Booyo, South Korea, during the Japanese occupation. He was 8 years old when the Korean Republic was established. He studied abstract painting at the University of Seoul. After his military service in divided Korea, he taught drawing at the Seminary of Seoul. In 1969, he left for Europe with a scholarship to the University of Fribourg in Switzerland, where he encountered the Dominicans and went on to become a priest in 1974. A year later, he moved to the Dominican monastery in Paris. Since then, Kim En Joong has exhibited his work all over the world, and is renowned for his paintings on glass windows. He is inspired by Vermeer, Rembrandt and Bonnard, as well as French Romanesque and Gothic art, Kandinsky and Rouault. In 2010, he was made an Officer of the prestigious Ordre des Arts et des Lettres.

MINES AND FLOWERS

You were born in South Korea, but are now living in Paris and enjoying international fame. What influence did your parents have on you?

They inculcated moral values in me. I was born during the Japanese occupation of my country in the Second World War. My father was a calligrapher, but could not make a living from that. I first saw electric light when I was 6 and my family was relocated to Taejon. I longed for an electric lamp in my room so that I could see the colours better in the magazines the Japanese left behind after the war.

Did you hate the Japanese occupiers?

Oh yes. The occupation was cruel, the country was plundered bare and we often went hungry. I was only a child, but I remember vividly how one day the Japanese brutally broke into our home and threatened my mother. Only much later, under the influence of Christianity, did it become clear to me that hate is not the right answer.

You started painting young!

Yes. I bought oil and powder and made the paint myself to save money. I made canvases from abandoned American sandbags that I sewed together and had a carpenter put on a frame. Much of what I produced at that time has been lost because I had no room to keep it. My work was discovered in 1962, and I was able to exhibit, but then I was called up for military service.

You went through tough military training.

Indeed. As you know, Korea is divided into two parts. Military service is compulsory and there is almost no way out of it. After my studies at the Fine Arts School in Seoul, I was appointed lieutenant and sent to the border area, where I served for two years. While there, I brushed shoulders with death. The border between North and South Korea is a river. Animals can cross it, but not people. 'Why not,' I wondered? I remember getting up at 5 o'clock one morning to climb a mountain. The landscape was gorgeous and I was struck by the colours of a clump of wild purple chrysanthemums in full bloom. When I bent to pick a few flowers, I suddenly noticed a mine among the stems. I was appalled! The contrast between the beauty of those flowers and the death contraption sobered my mood. I often thought about the meaning of life.

THE CROSS AND THE BUDDHA

Why did you become a Dominican?

Providence led me. Until I was 25, I had never heard of the Dominican Order. I lived only for my studies and to paint. Teaching drawing in the small seminary in Seoul, I was impressed by the quality of the seminarians. It's crazy, really – it wasn't the priests that inspired me, but their pupils!

Were you an atheist?

In the region where I was born in Korea, they believe in all kinds of spirits. When my grandfather died, every little hole in the house was plugged because the family was afraid that the spirits would come in. As a child, I found that frightening, as with everything to do with death. Traditionally, on 1 January, a meal is prepared for the family's dead, and everyone is sad. What's more, all the mountains and rivers have their own gods, who are always out for revenge and have no good intentions toward us humans. We had a rather sombre outlook on life.

That changed when I discovered the God of Christianity. The incarnation was a revelation to me – God made man! So totally different from Buddhism or Confucianism. The joy of Christians – especially at Easter – was quite new to me.

But what really freed me from the fear of death that had so plagued me was an article by Father Lelong about the death of Father Sertillanges, the great nineteenth-century Aquinas scholar. When he was supposed to say Mass and didn't appear, he was found dead at his desk. The ink of his last words was not yet dry. They were, 'Let us pray for each other and expiate our sins in brotherly fashion until we meet again in heaven.' They became important words for me. I know them by heart. They changed my life.

As an unbeliever, what attracted you to Christianity?

The celebration of Mass and the sacraments. That is where the physical exchange takes place between God-made-small and humans. We tend to imagine God as a mighty, all-powerful figure, but in the form of Jesus He became very small in order to move among us. To me, that's an incredible mystery, the absolute gentleness of God. A Buddhist or Confucian need not even betray his philosophy to become Christian, because Buddhism isn't a belief, but an ethical path that can gain in meaning through the Gospel. When I was in Japan, I met Vincent Shigeto Oshida, a Dominican who kept statues of the Buddha and Confucius beneath the cross. I loved that! He wanted to make the point that there is no contradiction between those philosophies and Christianity.

IN PARIS WITH ONLY 33 DOLLARS

When I left Seoul for Zurich, I bought a very cheap flight. But when I got to Hong Kong on the way, I couldn't board the plane because I didn't have the right visa. I could fly to Paris, but it would cost me another $77. So, I arrived at Orly airport with only $33. All I could think to do was to ask help from a priest. Like a cat on a mouse, I pounced on the first dog collar I saw. It turned out to be Monseigneur Morillon, the Bishop of Nantes! I had written on a piece of paper, 'Where can I spend the night in Paris for $33?' He immediately found a solution and took me to a mission in Paris. Later, I dedicated an exhibition to him in Nantes, by way of thanks. It always moves me to think of how that man cared for me like a good Samaritan.

Why did you choose the Dominicans?

When I arrived in Fribourg, I wanted to study at the Dominican university but that turned out to be really difficult. Just as I was about to give up, I came across the university's almoner, Brother Pfister. He helped me out, and I finally joined the Dominicans in 1970.

It was important to me that the Order had a positive attitude towards art. I was confirmed in my vocation by Brother de Menasce, who told me it was possible to be both priest and painter. He said, 'God respects what He endows on somebody. Keep going. Pray to Fra Angelico.' That first Dominican painter, who lived at the turn of the fifteenth century, shows that there is a long tradition of art walking hand in hand with spirituality. When I exhibited in the Hermitage Museum in 1989, I was able to admire the wonderful fresco by Fra Angelico depicting Mary, Thomas of Aquinas and Dominic. Before that fresco, I prayed that Leningrad would again become St Petersburg.

In one of your notes, you write, 'I return to Zurich not with my torch, as before, but with a small flame alight in my heart.'

When I arrived in Switzerland as a student, I took a job as a night watchman. I worked from half past nine in the evening until 6 o'clock in the morning. It meant patrolling the rich houses on a bike or motorbike, including the zoo, where the monkeys could be especially funny! What I remember from that period is the unnatural rhythm. When everybody else was asleep, I was working. During the day, I could sleep, but because I was so afraid of being late, I didn't manage to. It was a difficult period because I was so poor. And so I walked around the houses with my torch. In 1998, some 30 years after I first came there as a penniless student, I was invited to exhibit in Zurich. That time, I brought my canvases with me, as an ode to light in the creation.

Why did you want to become a priest?

It is the most beautiful offering. I was even prepared to give up painting for my priesthood, and that's really saying something! I have vivid memories of a powerful experience while walking in Seoul. It was impossible to deny that emotion, that call to become a priest, although I had not been baptized at the time. On the day of my ordination, I was inexpressibly happy: I could say Mass for the first time! I haven't missed one since. During Mass, I dedicate the whole world to God – even those who have hurt me.

THE LIGHT OF BRIOUDE

You say that you paint the way a bird sings. What do you mean?

I paint in a totally natural way. Marc Chagall said that if you are true to yourself, then painting comes naturally, but if you deviate from who you are, it goes wrong. Birdsong is very natural.

But how do you achieve that?

Before I start, I prepare myself in a number of ways. Like Michelangelo, I pray that my hand may be an instrument to reveal the mystery.

When I make stained-glass windows, another dimension comes in. When I was asked to make the windows for the basilica of St Julien de Brioude in Auvergne, I was afraid that the gorgeous church – a masterpiece of Romanesque art – would be too much for me. I visited it several times, sizing it up like a boxer weighing up his opponent before a bout. I didn't want to decorate this sacred space; rather, I wanted to reflect its essence with the help of my windows. I felt like a small instrument with a great ambition to make something beautiful, otherwise there's no point in beginning. When the first window was placed, to begin with I didn't dare look. But when I saw how the colourful window had succeeded in connecting the twelfth century to the twenty-first, I was delighted.

Is painting on glass more difficult than painting on canvas?

Yes, because the glass must go into the kiln, where it might crack. Working on glass is also more exciting, because you don't know quite how the light shining through will affect your work.

How, specifically, do you prepare yourself for your work?

I often get up in the middle of the night. When everything is quiet, I feel as if I am in the lap of the light. That gives me energy and nourishes my spirit. When I can't sleep, I read passages from the Gospels, stories of the saints or biographies of artists. What's amazing is that I feel completely happy when I go back to sleep. Before I set to work on a large canvas, I close my eyes and summon up the picture of a blue sky in which stars are appearing. Silence is very important. We Dominicans even say that silence is the father of preachers. It is our maxim. Also, when I paint there is a lot of space – space that is not empty, but full.

Is that typical Eastern thinking?

It is universal. St Dominic already stressed the importance of silence. In Korea, most Buddhist temples are located in the mountains, so that you have to prepare your inner state while climbing to reach them.

How has Western art influenced you?

Romanesque art is close to us Easterners. A Romanesque church could just as well be transformed into a Buddhist temple, because they emanate such simplicity and universality. With Gothic art and the Renaissance, you already feel a difference. Personally, I am seeking my own way. In the time that remains to me, I want to delve as deeply as possible into the catholic – meaning universal – in myself.

How do you see your task?

It isn't solely about what I want. It is God who shall lead me. It comes down to working and praying as much as possible. What the world needs is openness to the light, if I may put it like that. For me, that light is love, and points to the immortality of the soul. As an artist, my job is to make that inner light visible. The thirteenth-century Franciscan theologian Bonaventura said 'Light comes from God; colours come from the light.' I love bright colours and lines. You can use them to create a perfectly harmonious world.

Your paintings are abstract. Is there a reason for that?

Certainly, although I often sketch, too. But in my painting, I am seeking a transformation. I find that there is a surfeit of images: on the street, on television, in shops. I want to return to something that is more spiritual.

What do you do if you produce a painting that you're not satisfied with?

I burn it! A bad painting is like a corpse – you don't hold onto it.

What do you think of today's art?

I am very critical of many forms of modern art. The purpose of art is to bring peace. Many modern forms are too violent for my taste. I recently went to an important exhibition, but left quickly. It had nothing to do with art; it simply bore witness to pure chaos.

You're very scathing about modern art.

Precisely because of the violence. We already know enough about war and hate. Art must bring something else, something peaceful and harmonious.

Isn't that fleeing the world?

No, quite the opposite. It is hope-giving. I like to quote Dostoevsky, 'Beauty will save the world.' In fact, that is why I became a Christian. I am convinced that human beings are made in the image of God.

SELLING THE SOUL

You are in demand for many projects. Why don't you market your talents? With what you earn from your work, you could help the poor.

I could indeed earn a lot of money. But then I would have to sell my soul. Jesus said, 'The poor will always be with us.' I am not against wealth, but when making money is the only thing that matters, then the path lies open to dissolution and banality. Christ renounced every form of worldly success. Selling my paintings is not a goal in and of itself. I am convinced that if a painting has value, it will find its place.

How important are criticism and praise to you as an artist?

I love the reactions of ordinary people who buy a painting to use for their personal meditation. An Austrian couple wrote to me, 'When we leave for work in the morning, we always stand for a moment before your painting. And again in the evening.' A doctor from Nice who wanted a painting he could take with him whenever he travelled, bought one the right size. Last year, a group of Jews told me, 'Your work banishes the boundaries between your religion and ours.' That touched me deeply. These people pray in the presence of my work. That is the most beautiful praise I could receive, and these responses confirm my vocation as a painter. Fame does not interest me.

SOMETHING IS MISSING

Which values do you find important?

Those that are lasting, not subject to passing fads. The American violinist Isaac Stern once advised a student not to look at the audience when playing the violin. He stressed that it is important to be true to oneself and not to try to please the audience. I agree with this. It's important to be able to go against public opinion.

Why do people need to please others?

Because they are afraid: afraid of being alone, afraid of uncertainty. That is why Jesus so often says, 'Be not afraid, I am with you.' As an artist, whether you believe in God or not, you must go in search of an invisible world. Artists are called to build bridges between another world and our own.

Which invisible world are you speaking of?

We are only passing through, our sojourn here is temporary. When we die, that other reality breaks through – the one that art is pointing to. The role of art is to touch the soul. When you listen to the music of great composers like Bach and Beethoven, you hear something that transcends their time. My book Résonnances evokes letting God's spirit resonate within us, allowing contact between these two worlds.

In another book, Retrouvailles, I also refer to that invisible world. In the end, we must leave this world behind and greet death with joy, as St Francis says. Do you know the saying 'We paint because we are unhappy, we love music because we are sad'? I am not unhappy, certainly not when I paint, but nor am I fulfilled. Something is missing. I thirst for something, and only God can slake my thirst.

Have you ever been perfectly happy?

Almost – on the day I baptized my parents. I was ordained in Fribourg without their knowledge. My Order gave me permission to return to Korea for three months, and I planned to tell them then. When I arrived in Seoul, everyone was happy to see me. On the next day, my parents confided to me that they were looking for a wife for me. When I said that I was already married, because I had become a priest, my father was quiet for a long time and my mother wept. It came as a terrible shock to them. After a while, they accepted my choice, and then something unexpected happened: they asked me to help them to become Catholics too. At the end of my stay in Korea, I baptized them myself. At that moment I was almost perfectly happy.

THE VEIL TORN AWAY

Your good friend Father Lelong died in your arms. How has that affected you?

Father Lelong lay dying just as I returned from a long journey. I immediately went to his room, and we agreed that I would tidy it up 'for his beautiful death'. Because I was so tired, I went to bed, but he rang me at 5 in the morning. I confided to him that the terror I had always had of death was now gone. He echoed that feeling. Then I thanked him for everything he had done in his earthly life and said, 'We will meet each other yonder.' He answered strongly, 'Certainly!' That was his last word; then he died. It was one of the most important moments in my life. Since then, I have had the feeling that, at death, the veil is torn away and the passage is open.

15

Faustina Jimoh

Everything is within His knowledge

Nigeria is a divided country. With Christians in the south and Muslims in the north, where sharia law is imposed, this African country is often considered a front line of aggressive Islam. It is in the Islamic north that sister Faustina lives. I wonder what made her join the Dominican sisters in this rough environment when she was only 21.

As this is rather hostile territory for Christians, I expect the sisters not to wear their habits when they go into town, in the interests of their safety. So I am a little surprised when Faustina tells me that her sisters always wear the habit, and what's more, they feel at ease with it. Although they are occasionally called *Khafiri*, which means 'infidel', they also get positive comments about it. She explains, 'Surprisingly, if there is anything the Muslims like about us, it is the fact that we wear the habit. They see it as a decent way for a woman to dress and sometimes they wonder why other Christian women are not made to dress this way.'

At the time when sharia law was introduced, some taxis were designated for women, with drawings on them of women in *hijab*. As a result, a Dominican priest who is a chairman of the Christian Association of Nigeria questioned the state governor about why the drawing on the taxis was of a woman dressed in the Islamic way, when the taxis were meant for all woman, including Christians. The governor retorted that there are women in Christian churches who have their heads covered all the time, not seeming to understand that the habit denotes a particular way of life, and that it is not an obligation for other women.

Sister Faustina continues, 'Muslims wonder why we adopt this celibate lifestyle, which they see as a deprivation of self in many ways. Nonetheless, many Muslims respect us even though they are not at home with our religion.'

Like so many other Christians who are living as a minority in Muslim areas, this Dominican sister is confronted with the painful question, 'Stay or go?' I am curious to hear her answer.

Sister Faustina Jimoh was born in 1969 in Kabba, a town in Kogi, Nigeria. As a Dominican Sister, she worked in the Vicariate of Kontagora for about 12 years. During those years, she was engaged in women's development programmes, youth ministry, catechism and training people in primary evangelization. In 1998, she was sent to Ireland for further studies in information and communication technology and pastoral ministry. On her return to Nigeria in 2000, she was appointed Director of Religious Education for the Vicariate. Five years later, she was elected Prioress General of her congregation, the Dominican Sisters of St Catharine of Siena, in Gusau. In 2009, she was re-elected for another four years.

HOW WILL THEY KNOW?

What do you retain from your childhood?

The togetherness of my family was wonderful. We were a very happy family; not rich, but happy. I am the fourth of six children. My father was a builder and my mother a part-time trader, and they also had a farm. I loved the rainy season because everybody stayed at home when it rained and my mother would cook corn while my father told us stories. I remember coming home once with an award for being the best student in English language in my school. My parents, who had never been to school, were extremely happy and my father promised to do all he could to ensure that I could study to any length. It was one of the happiest moments in my life!

But I experienced some shocks as well. I never saw my parents disagree openly, but one night I awoke to hear my mother telling my father that she was going back to her mother's house and my father threatening to take her children from her if she did. I pleaded with my mum not to leave, and thank God she stayed. I was so shaken by that experience that it took me a while to reconnect with my father afterwards. My mother has always been a figure of major influence to me, I owe much to her positive outlook on life.

Why did you become a Dominican sister?

Because I wanted to preach! When I finished secondary school, I left the Catholic Church because I was not satisfied with the homilies and the lack of answers to my questions. I got involved with Pentecostalism while I was in the tertiary institution, but after about two years, something happened that made me turn around.

At school, there was a department for disabled people. I had often seen them, but, one day, as I was waiting to get into the lecture room, I was suddenly struck by two boys, one blind and the other lame, holding hands and helping each other on their way to the classroom. Suddenly, I heard a voice – I can't tell whether it came from inside me or outside – saying, 'How will people with these conditions know that God still loves them?' I stood pondering this for a long time, not realizing that all the students had gone into the hall until a friend came to see where I was. She saw me weeping, but I couldn't tell her what was wrong.

The question kept bothering me during the following vacation week, and then I made a commitment. I expressed to myself my desire to be sent to preach the word of God to those people. I was not thinking of becoming a nun or even a Catholic. But as I reflected more, I realized that if I got married I wouldn't be able to fulfil my desire. So what was I to do? Then I had a second experience, I heard that same voice again saying, 'You can only find what you are looking for in the Catholic Church.'

Deciding to return to the Catholic Church was a real struggle. I went back reluctantly, and eventually realized that my vocation was to become a sister. So I started looking for a congregation that would come closest to my desire to preach the word of God. I saw in the calendar of Missionaries of St Paul, a list of congregations and their charisms. When I saw, 'Dominicans, Order of

Preachers' it became crystal clear: 'Yes, that's what I am looking for!'

How did your family react?

I didn't have much support. Only my dad and one of my sisters were not opposed to my choice. It was very hard for my mother. She cried a lot and it took her a long time to accept my decision. She only came to the convent on the day I made my first vows.

Have you never had any doubts about this path? Don't you miss having a husband and children?

Well, yes, I do! When I was in formation, my friends used to write to me, saying they were having such a good time, encouraging me to forget about my vocation. 'You can serve God without locking yourself up,' they wrote. 'There is so much outside the convent!' And yes, I want to be married, I want to have children of my own. But at the end of the day, when I ask myself what is essential, I can only say that I still experience the passion to relate the love of God to people in whatever way.

What makes it all so hard is that we work in a very difficult region. The aridity of the land, the unfriendliness of many people, the Islamic environment is enough to make one leave. When I experience doubt, I ask myself, 'Why did I come here?' And I know it is because of the Dominican charism. If the Dominican charism changed, I would have a reason to leave. But it hasn't. I feel that there is something that God is calling me to give; God is opening my eyes to see. So it's beyond me, it's greater than myself.

NO INVITATION TO DIALOGUE

You are Prioress of your congregation. Can you describe the circumstances you live in?

We live in north-west Nigeria, in a region that is 99 per cent Islamic. It's tough because it's not an environment that invites dialogue. Co-existence is the only thing that we hope will stay attainable.

So, it's difficult in terms of religion, in terms of climate, in terms of the widespread poverty. We are not able to generate enough income to look after ourselves and our ministry as preachers. Most of the people who send their children to our school cannot afford to pay fees. I worry a lot about how to meet our daily financial needs; the need for food, shelter, health care, education.

We are still very dependent on the support of our sisters in the United States, but it is important for us to become self-reliant. Apart from that, what is most challenging for us is to look constantly for ways to befriend the Islamic community. Sometimes I think the Muslims would be happier if we left, even though they benefit from our services. They obviously like the education they are getting from our schools, but they still can't give us the freedom to operate as we would like to. We are deprived of our rights as Christians.

What kind of deprivation are you referring to?

I'll give you an example. When the Great Bend Dominican Sisters who founded our congregation came to Gusau in 1956, they built a convent, a maternity ward and a dispensary. In the 70s, the government took over the maternity ward and dispensary. In the years that followed, they even tried to evict the sisters from their home. Although some of those properties have been returned, the Gusau local government is still not ready to hand back everything. Because of the small dispensary inside our domain, which they claim is theirs, they have refused to let us complete the wall around our convent. The next thing they did was to apportion the land in front of the dispensary to some of their people to build lock-up shops. We contested this plan because if we let them build shops, a mosque inside our compound would probably be next. So we took them to court. For eight years we struggled in court over our property. Eventually, we won the case three times in the local court, but now they have appealed to a higher court and we are still waiting for what that might bring.

Zamfara was the first state in Nigeria to introduce sharia law. Are you as Christians subject to this law as well? Do Christians automatically become dhimmis, second-class citizens, under sharia law?

When sharia was introduced, we were told it would not affect Christians, but it definitely has. For example, the motorcycles we use as a means of transport were suddenly subject to sharia rules, namely that no woman should be found on a motorbike driven by a man. Then some taxis were provided 'for women only', but as no woman was allowed to sit in the front, next to the male driver, all women were cramped in the back. The rules are meant for everybody, Christians and Muslims alike. There were other issues too, like dress code and buying, selling or drinking alcohol. Some of these rules are now ineffective, such as the use of bikes. Being an Islamic environment, a Christian is always suspected of proselytizing, and a Christian may not easily secure a job unless he is willing to convert to Islam.

How many sisters are there in your mother house and what kind of work are they engaged in?

There are currently 10 sisters and 11 novices. Some of us are engaged in teaching and others in administrative work, but as a congregation, our apostolates include schools, hospitals, pastoral, social and rural-development work.

Do you also reach Muslims in your schools and projects? What's your policy about hijab, the traditional head covering for Muslim women?

We do not discriminate against anyone, no matter their religious affiliation. We welcome whoever comes to us, but unfortunately we have experienced resistance from some Muslim families whom we have invited to benefit from our project for disabled children for fear that we would convert them. It takes a while before some begin to trust our intention.

On the issue of *hijab*, there has been a move to make us introduce its use for girls in some of our schools, but we have refused because these are mission schools. However, we reached a compromise by introducing the use of berets instead. We are also not allowed to teach Christian religious knowledge in our schools unless we are prepared to teach Islamic religious knowledge too.

What have been the most difficult situations you have encountered so far?

The most difficult is the precarious situation in which we live – not knowing what will happen to us next, whether we will live or die the next minute or day. Our mother house is constantly guarded by police because there could be riots. When there is tension in another part of the country, we experience the tension too, because things might escalate easily.

The local emir of the town where our house is situated enjoys great honour as an Islamic leader. We have been told that he has played an important role in warding off religious fundamentalism in the town so far. But he is old now and we are worried about what might happen when he is no longer there. Some time last year there was violence in Sokoto town, where we have two communities. The sisters had to be evacuated to the army barracks for a few days. This is what I mean: today may be fine, tomorrow may be dramatic, we don't know.

If things are that volatile, why don't you leave?

We were founded to be a Christian presence in northern Nigeria. Leaving would mean abandoning our mission and that would affect the few Christians remaining, especially the indigenous ones who might no longer be able to practise their faith and might be compelled to become Muslims. I know the seed of Christianity has been sown and it can't end that easily, but it would be the end of a certain Christian presence in north-west Nigeria. We want to bear witness to the love of God.

But Islam also refers to love.

Yes, and that could unite us and create the openness to be able to live together.

Why not convert to Islam if both religions hold love central?

It has to do with conviction. You and I may have the same cloth to make a dress, but the choice of style is up to each one individually. I want to bear witness to the love of God as a Christian. I was born a Christian, I did not choose it from the start of my life but I came to choose it as I grew up. I have encountered God through the Christian faith.

What have been the best experiences during your time as Prioress?

What has given me the most joy in my 20 years in the convent and in my fifth year in leadership is the sisters themselves. When I think of their inner strength, the joy they radiate, hanging on in spite of everything and giving their very best in whatever they do, then I am even more convinced that God wants us to be here.

Why do young girls join the Dominican sisters when Nigeria is giving them such a hard time?

First, I won't say that in general it is difficult to be a sister in Nigeria. In other parts of the country, life is much easier in terms of freedom to express one's faith.

When young girls want to join our community, I tell them first about the financial difficulties, the Islamic environment and the harsh climate. We live close to the desert, so it is either very hot or extremely cold, and it's dry and dusty. The situation is different in the middle belt or parts of the country where there is no religious crisis and where the climate is mild. What drives us to this desert is beyond what anybody can explain. We are like missionaries in our own country.

Is there a Gospel story that you like more than others?

The story that comes to me readily is when Jesus was in the boat with His disciples during the storm. They thought He was sleeping. The wind and waves were tossing them around and they woke up Jesus because they were afraid. At that time, they probably did not understand who He was. So He had to perform the miracle of calming the sea, and thus moving them from one level of faith to another, assuring them of His presence.

Sometimes, in very difficult circumstances, I close my eyes and say to myself, 'God, I believe that you are here.' I have realized that I don't have to keep running around. If I run to America and there is crisis, then I run to Europe. If there is crisis in Europe, where do I run to next? It has to reach a point where I must stop, where I must recognize that whatever happens *here* or *there*, it is within His knowledge.

16

Breda Carroll

DROGHEDA, IRELAND

A white building atop a hill

The austere building overlooking the town of Drogheda in Ireland looks to me very modern and a bit cold, but I am given the warmest of welcomes by sister Breda. Dominican nuns are poor, but local people bring them meat and fish, which they enjoy only on feasts, besides serving them to guests like me. I am embarrassed by their generosity.

Wooden sculptures, icons, a harp, a zither, richly coloured glass windows by the Dominican painter Kim En Joong make this place holy and beautiful. Yet it is the presence of the nuns in their choir stalls that imbues the atmosphere with quiet. The heart of their prayer is the daily celebration of the liturgy in the presence of the Exposed Blessed Sacrament. No more than a little piece of bread surrounded by the golden flames of the monstrance, no less than Christ himself.

During my stay, sister Breda will be my guide, answering all my questions, never getting fatigued or annoyed. Even when I ask critical questions: 'Aren't you fleeing from the world? Why don't you call for women priests? Isn't living in a monastery useless?'

Once, during the daily praying of the rosary at noon, a middle-aged man walked in and was touched by what was going on. He began to weep aloud. A bankrupt businessman, it seemed that he had resolved to commit suicide but, knowing there was a monastery on top of the hill, he decided he might as well have a look there first. And then the unexpected happened.

Healing – deep healing – is what all kinds of people passing through the gate are longing for. And it sometimes happens that the silence speaks to them in quite unforeseen ways.

Breda Carroll was born in 1950 in Tralee, County Kerry in south-west Ireland. She became a Dominican nun when she was 18. She is currently the Prioress of the only monastery of Dominican nuns in Ireland, St Catherine of Siena in Drogheda.

IN NO CONVENT!

You grew up on a farm. What memories do you retain?

We were happy although we had very little. We didn't have a phone, a television or a car, for instance. As a family, we rarely did anything together because we had a small dairy farm and cows needed to be milked morning and evening. Holidays were spent helping my dad make hay and do other jobs around the farm. My parents were not outspokenly religious, although my father would always kneel down in the kitchen after breakfast and say his prayers.

When did the idea of wanting to become a nun take root in your heart?

I always wanted to be a missionary, perhaps because I had read the missionary magazines at school. For a long time, I carried this tremendous desire in my heart to become a nun. When I was a teenager I tried to tell my mother that I was interested in becoming a nun, but she never took me seriously and always answered, 'You'll be kept in no convent!' as I could sometimes be a bold and angry child.

Why did you want to devote yourself to contemplation?

When I was 16, while listening to the news on the Vietnam War, I suddenly became aware that if I were a missionary, it might not fulfil my expectations, maybe I would be confined to just one little spot. At that moment, something within me said, 'The best way to be missionary is to be a contemplative.' It was something very real that happened to me and I answered, 'Yes Lord, if you show me the way.' But I didn't speak to anybody about it as I was too afraid and didn't know any contemplative communities.

When I got a job in Dublin, I asked advice from a Dominican priest who served in St Saviour's Church. He sent me down to

Drogheda and once I met the community, I was convinced! I felt drawn to give myself unreservedly to God in silence and solitude and precisely by so doing to make Him known and loved throughout the world. Two seemingly contradictory ideals, but the holding together of them is the very essence of our identity as Dominican nuns. When I finally told my mother, she said she didn't like the idea of my being enclosed in a monastery (we had double grills at that time) so far away from home.

I was scared to death to go inside those grills, but I felt this was the price to pay. My dad said, 'Do what you want to do and we will support you.' When I look back, I realize that they would have been glad of some financial support, but at 18 one does not think beyond oneself! They gave me the freedom to follow my vocation and I'm eternally grateful for that.

Were you allowed to leave the monastery to visit your family?

I came in with the understanding that there was no getting out. But things changed in the Church around that time. Before receiving the habit and beginning my novitiate, I was able to visit my parents, and they saw that I was happy. Afterwards, I went home occasionally, and when my parents got older and handed the farm over to my brother, they visited more often.

During my stay in the monastery, I sometimes sneaked into church and noticed there were always a few nuns sitting in silence while a monstrance was displayed on the altar. The intensity of it reminded me of the silent Zen meditation I attended in Japan with Father Oshida. What is the meaning of this 'adoration' and why is the monstrance displayed on the altar?

The word 'adoration' is used to describe the highest praise we offer to our God. Our community is dedicated to Eucharistic adoration – prayer before the Blessed Sacrament – both in the tabernacle and exposed in the monstrance on the altar.

Before Mass, the Blessed Sacrament stays hidden in the tabernacle. We believe that the bread and wine become the body and blood of Jesus at Mass and that continues after Mass. A piece of this transformed bread is put into a monstrance, and this is exposed on the altar until after evening prayer. The exposed Blessed Sacrament is surrounded with candles, lights and flowers as tokens of reverence and respect. Being visible, unlike the Eucharistic bread in the tabernacle, it appeals more to the senses. We believe that this is the sacramental presence of the risen Jesus.

We begin adoration at 5 in the morning and continue until 10.30 in the evening. Each of us is assigned approximately two hours of Eucharistic adoration daily, but we are free to spend more time. The aim of our life is to foster continuous prayer. Personally, I hesitate to tie down our prayer to a certain number of hours. What is important is this continuous prayer of the heart. Some sisters who manage their work time well can allow themselves much more free time than others. So, some sisters may spend less time in formal prayer, but in fact they may be praying continuously in their hearts!

What does it mean to pray in your heart?

Prayer is the simplest thing in the world and it's the most difficult. Techniques can help prepare the ground, but prayer is ultimately God's gift. All Christian prayer springs from the fact that through baptism we are 'in Christ'. St Paul says, 'We cannot say Jesus is Lord unless we are under the influence of the Holy Spirit.' It is the Spirit who prays in us. Our job is to remove the obstacles. I love the saying by St Augustine, 'You have made us for yourself, O Lord and our heart is restless until it rests in you.'

How do you pray?

That's very difficult to say. Prayer is not an achievement, it's not just kneeling down saying prayers. Prayer is a relationship, a 'being with' the one who we know loves us. It also implies engaging with my own weaknesses, my own sinfulness; trying to bring the deepest part of my heart into conformity with God's will. We believe that when we gather to say the Divine Office, we are united with the whole church. We are praying in the name of the whole church and Christ is among us.

I especially like the Latin word *hodie*, meaning 'today'. What we are doing in the Eucharist is not just commemorating something from the past. On the contrary, redemption is happening now. For instance, in the liturgy at Christmas, we often repeat, 'Today Christ is born, today angels rejoice!' Each morning at the start of the Office, we say, 'O, that today you would listen to His voice.' The word 'today' when used in our liturgy signifies that salvation is taking place now.

In using the word 'today' when referring to events in the past, like Christmas, you seem to refer to another dimension of time.

Yes, faith teaches us another, mysterious dimension.

I wonder what leads you into contemplative silence.

Sometimes just reading the scripture, walking around in the garden and observing the beauty of nature, the flowers and the birds or getting in touch with my breathing. A great privilege is being in the presence of the Exposed Blessed Sacrament. We don't use any special techniques. Sometimes I use the Jesus prayer and just repeat, 'Jesus be merciful to me, sinner' or I just repeat the word 'Jesus'.

Do you expect results from your prayers?

Prayer is an experience of faith. It is not about seeing results. However, we frequently hear of wonderful answers to prayers. I think it's good to bear in mind that we ourselves are the worst judges of our prayer. I could spend a very distracted hour with the Lord and another day I could have very good feelings. But maybe the time when I am just struggling might be the time that is most fruitful. Prayer is not about having good feelings, sometimes prayer can be a struggle, it can be darkness.

DARKNESS OF FAITH

During prayer times, I was touched by the harmony, beautiful singing and peace emanating from the liturgy. Where is the darkness you speak about?

The darkness of faith. The Lord can be absent for most of the time, but through my faith I know He is also present in the darkness. I didn't come to the monastery just to be able to have good feelings in prayer. I'm attracted and drawn to prayer, but I don't see my function in the monastery as having peace and quiet.

What do other people gain from it when you suffer darkness?

All of us are linked in the mystical body of Christ. It's the image St Paul uses in his letter to the Corinthians when he says that if his little finger is hurting the whole of him feels the pain. He uses the same image in his letter to the Colossians where he says, 'I make up in my body what is lacking in the death of Christ.' We know that Jesus' death is complete and that we don't have to save the world, but somehow He allows us to share in His passion because we are all incorporated into Him. The Lord lets some of us experience a bit of darkness so that others can be out of the pain. There is so much suffering in the world; we don't come to the monastery to protect ourselves from that. All of us have our wounds; it is the purification that causes the darkness and is painful.

Haven't you ever doubted your faith?

Oh yes, yes. But I deal with it by just making an act of faith. By saying, 'Lord, I do believe. I want to believe.'

But don't you need a personal experience to go on?

I have very few experiences. I am not one of those people who experiences the Lord very vividly. Sometimes I envy people that have these very good experiences of the Lord; I have had nothing like that. No, it's more a conviction, an inner sense, but it is very strong and it guides me through. If I doubt, I just go back to that moment when I first experienced the Lord's call to monastic life. I still feel that this is what the Lord wants of me and it has brought me much joy.

You also engage in lectio divina. *What does it mean?*

Lectio divina literally means sacred reading – it is a term used in particular for a prayerful reading of sacred scripture. We ponder God's word and reflect on it, not just at times of *lectio divina*, but throughout the day the scripture reverberates. We also do *lectio divina* as a community. Each week, we read the Gospel after night prayer on Monday night and we spend ten minutes in silence. On Wednesday nights we read it again and we pass around a microphone. Each sister is free to mention a phrase or a word that strikes her. On Saturdays, we come together and we share how our *lectio* has spoken to each of us. We have become closer as a community through this practice.

Do you chat with each other in the monastery?

We try to maintain a prayerful atmosphere of silence throughout the monastery. If we need to discuss something, we are always free to do so. Normally we come together for 45 minutes daily recreation. During this time we chat or play games. We can watch the news once a day, but we often just read the daily papers instead.

Isn't it difficult when you have to interrupt you work to go to church? Don't you ever get bored?

In one sense it is difficult because it breaks up the day. On the other hand, it means that we are always reminded of our vocation to adore and praise God and intercede for the Church and the world. It also stresses the fact that each section of the day is sanctified.

I don't get bored because liturgy is what gives variety to our life. It is a living thing. It's not about the words, but about the mystery that is happening 'now'. Year after year, the mystery deepens because it is too big for us to understand in one go. Many people ask us, 'What do you do for Christmas?' I answer, Christmas is our celebration of the liturgy. Liturgy is our Christmas!'

COMPLETELY USELESS

Monasteries are often criticized for being useless places. But Pope Benedict XVI has compared monasteries to the green lungs of a city – beneficial to all even if people don't know they exist. And Timothy Radcliffe adds that your lives are completely useless and that's exactly the purpose! What kind of reactions do you get?

The young sisters who have joined us indeed get criticized for wasting their lives. But I am convinced that prayer reaches out, even if nobody knows us. People are touched through prayer. We create an empty space. We are continually listening to the word and let it take root in our hearts so that others may hear. There is a constant stream of people who come here to sit and pray or ask our prayers for various problems.

Isn't it rather egotistical to sit and pray and not engage in social work like giving bread and soup to the poor?

It might look like that, but in today's world people may be more in need of spiritual bread and soup. There is a deep spiritual hunger among people.

How can cloistered nuns be members of the Order of Preachers? Do you go out and preach?

No, but it depends on what you mean by preaching. The very fact that the monastery exists is a preaching in itself. If God does not exist, we are fools. The greatest preaching is to make people think about God. The prayerful celebration of the liturgy is a powerful preaching and our chapel door is always open, from before morning prayer until after evening prayer for those who wish to join us in prayer. Prayer is at the heart of preaching, so, in this sense, we are preachers. In addition, we try to spread the word through our printing department and writing of icons.

NUNS, SHOW US THE ORDER!

What is the nuns' connection to St Dominic?

He is our father and founder. Unlike other orders of nuns, we don't have a mother foundress – St Dominic himself is our sole Master. He was the teacher of the first nuns, who were gathered in Prouille ten years before the confirmation of the Order in 1216. I like those stories of Dominic walking down late at night to Prouille to teach the nuns. It shows his love and concern for the nuns, which is probably unique to our Order. Later, he entrusted the nuns to the care of the friars and for the past 800 years there has been this close bond between the nuns and the friars who provide them with spiritual and intellectual formation. All the recent masters of the Order – Brother Damien, Brother Timothy, Brother Carlos – have been wonderful to the nuns.

What also appeals to me about Dominic is that he points away from himself to Jesus. No popular devotion grew up around Dominic, as it did around other saints. Dominic always turns us towards somebody greater, a bit like John the Baptist did.

'Nuns, show us the Order' is an oft-quoted saying by the previous Master of the Order, Carlos Aspiroz. What does it mean?

Historically, it refers to the words of Dominic, who called on the nuns of Prouille to teach the nuns of a new foundation in San Sisto in Rome what contemplative life was about. Today, it refers to the contemplative dimension of the Order. In recent years, Brother Carlos and Brother Timothy have worked very hard to bring back that contemplative dimension, as there is always a tendency to become overactive. The nuns' way of life is a constant reminder of the contemplative dimension of the Order.

Who is God to you?

God has always been very real for me, even as a child. God capti-vated my heart at a very young age and I can still feel that sense of being grasped by Him. I can't explain it. All I know is that it is something real for me. On another level, I can say that I don't know Him at all, that I feel as if I have no intimate relationship with Him and that I am *not* close to Him. Ultimately, I see God as the one from whom I come and the one to whom eventually I will go.

I was influenced by Walter J. Ciszek's book *He Leadeth Me*. He was a Polish priest who was imprisoned and who denied the Lord at one moment. Afterwards he had a lightning bolt of insight that God's will is not something out there that he needed to achieve but that God's will is in the circumstances someone finds himself in. So, I can find Him in the kitchen, in whatever I am supposed to do right now.

A MOST DIFFICULT TRUTH

This monastery is named after Catherine of Siena who was proclaimed a Doctor of the Church and was a lay Dominican. Helen Alford, a dean of the Angelicum, also refers to her decisive influence on the popes and clergy of the fourteenth century. Are you inspired by her?

For a long time, I was turned off by Catherine of Siena because I saw her as this extraordinary figure who did all these penances and was in ecstasy for most of her life. I never saw her as a model until I began reading her texts, especially the Dialogue. She puts into words what could be seen as the heart of Dominic, who has left us no works apart from one letter. Catherine is very confident in the merits of Christ's redemption. She turns to the Eternal Father, she almost tells Him what to do, namely to have mercy on the world. That cry for mercy is something that finds an echo in every Dominican heart. While he was still a Canon of St Augustine, Dominic's prayer was for true charity which would enable him to work for the salvation of souls. The Church in Catherine's day was every bit as bad, or even worse, than in our own. Her teaching on prayer is always linked with charity, which is love.

She has the Father saying to her in the Dialogue that He wants us to exercise the same kind of love with which He has loved us – gratuitously, without expecting anything back. Then He adds that we can't give Him the same kind of love, but we can give that love to our brothers and sisters. So, we have to walk with two feet – love of God and love of neighbour. In doing so, we are dependent on one another, because the other person supplies us with what we lack.

What did she mean by 'self-knowledge' in her day?

Self-knowledge is not to be understood in terms of psychological knowledge of oneself. It means knowing how much we are loved by God. I think it's one of the most difficult truths to grasp: that I, personally, am loved by God. I can believe it of everybody else, but not of myself. And in speaking to others, I have come to see that it is a common problem. Everybody has the feeling of not being loved, even if one comes from the best of families and has many talents. It seems that love in its perfection can't be experienced. Nobody can give us perfect love except God, but we first need human love to experience it. It is something we can only become aware of gradually.

How can this gap in one's heart be healed?

It varies for different people. Our image of God is often coloured by our human experience. Being accepted by other people is wonderfully healing. It has helped me a great deal. Self-acceptance gives one the power to change. That's where prayer and *lectio divina* come in. God is always at work. The child thinks it learns to walk by itself, forgetting that it is the parents who are leading it. Acceptance of ourselves and realizing that God is present in whatever happens, is healing. I'm convinced that if we could only once grasp His love for us, we could do great things.

What about women as priests?

The question has never been raised in our community, but I understand that some sisters are angry at not being allowed to become priests. I personally think that men and women have different roles. It's not about being superior or inferior, but about complementing one another. God chose a woman to bear His Son without needing a man. That puts a woman on a very high level because she and she alone brought Jesus onto the world!

What is your favourite Gospel story?

At the Last Supper, Jesus gives us a wonderful insight into His own heart and mind and His relationship with the Father: 'On that day, you shall know that I am in my Father, and you in me, and I in you.' And: 'I am the vine, you are the branches. Whoever remains in me with me in him bears fruit in plenty, for cut off from me you can do nothing.' I like the idea that Jesus is living His life again in me, as St Therese of Lisieux says, 'Jesus, you have given us an impossible command, namely to love others as you love them. But since you can't command me to do something impossible, you have to come and live through me.' I try to live that, in the sense that when somebody is upset, I call on Jesus and ask Him to come and show love through me so that the other person can be comforted.

NO MERIT, ONLY JOY

You have been living here for more than 40 years now. What has been your greatest sorrow?

(*After a long silence*) That sense of disappointment of not always having responded as generously as I desire. God is always present, but sometimes I am not with Him. I'm not always fine-tuned to His presence.

What has been your greatest joy?

The joy of being here. If I had to start over, I would choose it again. The words that come to my mind are those of Blessed Reginald, quoted by Blessed Jordan of Saxony in his book the *Libellus* that tells the story of the foundation of the Order. He says that he had no merit because he experienced such joy to be in the Order. I can identify with those words: I love liturgy, Eucharistic adoration, community life. Living in community, which hasn't always been painless, has brought me great joy because we are basically a united community. I often wonder why God chose me from an insignificant family and an insignificant background to enter a monastery. I can only marvel at God's goodness to me.

17

Vincent Shigeto Oshida

I shall meet you in Galilee

'He knows.' The Japanese friar directs his penetrating gaze at me and says, 'He knows your needs before you express them. Did He not know that the wine was finished before His mother told Him so?'

This eastern Dominican friar, Vincent Shigeto Oshida, is headstrong, profound and poor. So headstrong that his superiors in Canada finally gave him his way and allowed him to return to his roots, to found a community here that would be both Japanese and Christian. Here in the village Takamori Soan, there are no entry restrictions. Everyone can come and go, because everyone carries Christ within.

The ground rule of the people living here, in huts built of construction waste and cardboard, is poverty. There are no possessions, everything is received from the Lord or from the neighbouring farmers. It seems to be a precondition for happiness.

Oshida is sick. His health never recovered fully after nearly drowning at the age of 26, but this trial also opened his way to deeper insight. He has become a sought-after speaker the world over, and even organized the Asian Bishops' Conference at his community. Fasting and prayer are the focus. The prelates didn't know what to think – only later did it strike them: 'We are all too rich.'

Mass is celebrated by candle light in a wooden hut on stilts. Prayer is very focused. You can feel the spirit of Zen wedded to the spirit of Christ. Oshida calls himself 'a Buddhist who has met Christ'. Some twigs are burning in an iron pot to the murmur of a prayer to the Holy Ghost. The flames crackle up to the roof, but I'm the only one who watches them, amazed. The rest are sunk in silence. Outside, night is falling and the only light is coming from the moon.

Fujiyama watches majestically over this small community. The mountain is overpoweringly huge, and yet it also seems vulnerable when its summit is shrouded in mist. Power and fragility are mingled in the mountain – just as they are in this man.

Vincent Shigeto Oshida was born in 1922 in Yokohama, Japan, into a Buddhist-Shinto family. He read philosophy at the University of Tokyo, and went on to study theology in Canada, where he joined the Dominican order. Back in Japan, in Takamori Soan – a village at the foot of Mount Fuji – he founded a community based on poverty, Zen meditation and life in nature. This pioneer of interreligious dialogue was truly recognized when the Asian Bishops' Conference was held in his village in 1990. He died in 2003 and was buried in Takamori.

FEAR OF STARS

What has stayed with you from your childhood?

When I was 6, I used to sit next to my father as he practised *zazen* (meditation) every day. I learned to meditate in much the same way as I learned to eat rice with chopsticks. It was something very natural.

As a child, I was afraid of looking at the stars, because I was haunted by the question of what lay behind them. I thought I would go mad, and felt myself surrounded by this mystery.

At night, I would cry from fear of dying and what came after. My parents understood none of this. In my 20s, I first met a truly spiritual person – the Jesuit father Hoybers, a free man in whom I sensed Christ. 'Your vocation is clear,' he said simply. I got baptized and wanted to become a priest, so I went to Canada.

THE BREATH OF GOD

What events have influenced you?

When I was 26, something happened that changed my life. It happened in Canada, while I was out swimming with other seminarians. I was saved from drowning, just in the nick of time. When I was drawn from the water, my body was already quite rigid and they thought I was dead. But my friend, a Canadian brother, couldn't accept that all attempts to save me had been abandoned and so he marched in desperation to a nearby village, found an iron rod and wrenched my mouth open so he could give me the breath of life. What nobody thought possible happened: I regained consciousness and survived.

That's when my calvary started in earnest. My lungs were so damaged from lack of oxygen that one of them had to be removed. And it didn't stop there: things got so bad that the doctors decided to give up treatment. I lay at death's door a second time. And again, I was miraculously saved! One way or another, I survived in the conviction that I could not die and leave behind the Church as a bastion of the bourgeoisie! My ideal was the priesthood, even if I could only say Mass once. So I went to a priory. The prior, the second spiritual person I met, was a Dominican. He asked me if I thought I could ever give up a career as an intellectual or artist to pursue a spiritual life. I was full of doubt, and wondered what means of expression would be left to me if I did so. In the end, after a few months, I accepted my calling. Since then I have been following the hand of God. Often, at the time, you don't understand what is happening. It only becomes clear later on.

Is that a trust you live from?

It is belief. My life is based on the conviction that God knows and will provide what is needed. I have reached the conclusion that it is not possible to make long-term plans in this life. All you have to do is meet the needs of the moment. If you make plans, you are creating your own world, and then the free sphere in which you can enter into dialogue with God disappears.

Here in Takamori Soan the wind has never stopped blowing. It is *souffle*, the breath of the hereafter, the other world. But it would be many years before this community would be born.

When I finally decided to become a Dominican, my weak body fell into difficulties again. We had to get up in the middle of the night to pray, and I was of course the first to fall sick and had to return to hospital. And then something even worse happened: I got the feeling that I had lost the most valuable gift I had ever been given – God's mercy. This was a black time for me. It was aggravated by memories floating up on my sickbed from my work during the war, when I organized alms of food for the poor in Tokyo. Suddenly I realized that it hadn't been the breath from the other world that had driven me, but the whiff of my own ego! It was shattering to see that I had lived my whole life in the sign of selfishness. I knew that I had to snuff out my ego if I was ever to be able to live a spiritual life. When I recovered and returned to the priory, my fear of death became very intense. And yet my drowning experience gave my fear a different tinge. I began to sense the hereafter, as if I had been given an all-embracing glimpse and understood that everything is entrusted to God.

The prior of the seminary noticed this and invited me to his room. His words made a deep impression on me: 'What you are tasting is what theology calls *sapientia* – wisdom.' He sensed what lived in me. When I hear birdsong, I feel the hereafter; I hear the deepest voice of God, not mingled with my own voice or the voice of society. The child Shigeto, the adult and the old man are present here, inseparably bound to Him, sometimes touched by His presence. God's breath is always there.

TAKAMORI SOAN

How did this community come to be?

My whole life is a continual process of illness. Once, while I was again lying in hospital, I had a sudden, important insight: a truly spiritual life must start from absolute poverty.

I decided to live in solitude as a hermit, *and* as a Christian *and* as a true Japanese. In the beginning, I lived alone in an abandoned Buddhist temple. The Dominicans in Canada didn't understand my way of life, but they helped me to build a hut from cardboard and construction waste. To my astonishment, many people turned up wanting to live in the same way! We bought some very cheap land in Takamori Soan, a village where I felt the old Japanese culture, and the community grew. There came a time when everything had been used up – money and materials. We didn't know what to do. But next day, people came from the village with spontaneous offers of help. And that's how it's always gone. There have been only two occasions when we had no money and nothing to eat, and we felt so happy! At last, we had nothing! But that didn't last long, because the following day someone set some vegetables on the table. Who? I still don't know, but we learned something very important: God gives you what you need, and when you're poor, you are constantly aware of this. To be poor is to find yourself in the hand of God.

A TENDER HEART

Is poverty really a precondition for a spiritual life?

Someone who has money or knowledge doesn't really know how to give of himself. It comes down to getting free of every position you have. How else can you talk with the living beings around you; with stones, earth, water? When it freezes, the water freezes. When it thaws, the ice melts.

That is spirituality, the maternal spirituality of the earth, but we no longer understand anything about it. The use of chemical fertilizers kills the earth and the quality of our rice is diminishing.

We call that *civilization*, and we think we understand how it works. But it's not something to be understood with the intellect. Rather, you need the insight that harming one single living being also harms other living beings! Really, it's not about the mind, but the heart. I often think back to the best time in my life, just after the War. Everyone was hungry, but everyone was so gentle with each other. Your heart must be tender to be able to feel another's suffering. If you can do that, you are truly human. You can't learn tenderness at university, you can only learn it from other, seasoned people.

What rules do visitors have to follow?

We have only one rule: that we carry the cross of another as if it were our own. We live in solidarity with Christ and each other. At harvest time, we go into the paddy fields with the villagers. Work is seen not merely as a means to earn a living – it is also spiritual practice. Everyone who comes here is welcome, because they are sent by God. We pray, work and eat together. There are separate huts, but we possess nothing of our own. When I came to live here, my brother wanted to give me money, but I refused because money is not our objective.

DHYANA

Why do people come here?

God, providence, contemplative life, Zen, *dhyana*. When I use the word 'Zen', I don't just mean Zen Buddhist meditation. I use the word in its original meaning: *dhyana*, the Sanskrit word for Zen meditation. In China it is translated as *ch'an*, in Japan as Zen. I use it with a specific meaning, namely, Zen is the way of *reality*; to experience that reality, not to chat about it! For me, that reality is inseparable from the revelation of Jesus Christ, and I explore that reality through Zen. Our visitors are probably attracted by that orientation.

Is the intellect important in opening someone to that reality?

(*Fiercely*) Absolutely not! Using the mind is no help at all! I am talking about a totally different world. It has nothing, absolutely nothing to do with study! You have to open yourself up! It cannot be learned through intellect, through the *word-idea*. Only a master can break through this mental conditioning, not someone who has received only university training. Involvement with other living beings, acceptance of responsibility is important. In that sense, you can only learn through your own experience, doubt and questioning. Why are Westerners so slow to understand this?

Which is more important: meditation or action?

This distinction is drawn by the intellect. If you think in terms of opposites, that is a sign that you are living at a very superficial level. No action without contemplation! No contemplation without action! The two are inseparably entwined.

What is your liturgy like in Takamori Soan?

Every morning at 5 o'clock, we practise *zazen* in our small chapel, which is built like a simple Japanese country house. Zen rituals are performed in the zendo, not in the chapel. Next come morning prayers. We take the time for liturgy, and we read the scriptures at a very slow pace. The psalms are not sung, but murmured. After breakfast, we work in silence until lunchtime. In the afternoon we take a short rest, after which we carry on working until 5 o'clock Mass. Mass is performed in the same measured, meditative fashion. There used to be an altar in the chapel, but after my journey to India I replaced it with a small wooden block. I wanted to get closer to the earth, and decided to simply sit on the ground to celebrate Mass. We replaced the collection box with an iron pot where we burn twigs as a symbol of the offering. After supper, we sometimes read the Bible in a contemplative way. The day ends with evening prayers at 8.30.

THE ACTION-HAND OF GOD

What specific difference do you see between West and East?

Words are not there to be understood, but to incite action! The word must denote a direct contact with reality. To express this dynamic, I call the process *word-event*. People think that word is the same as concept, but that is not so! The word is the action-hand of God. You can learn a lot here from the insects and animals. One cold winter's night in my hut, I felt something crawl over my chest. It was a rat that was so cold it came looking for the warmth of my blankets. I realized that the creature shared the same reality as us; the same cold, too. The next morning, it had vanished, but at least it had spent the night in the warm.

By contrast, intellectual thinking – what I call *word-idea* – is typically European. Who are we to divide the Bible, for example, into chapters on the basis of our perspective, our intellectual way of thinking? 'He who is always hidden' is everywhere. Our contact with the world must be direct, not mediated by ideas manufactured by the intellect.

To understand this, you must become poor: a pilgrim in life with empty hands but free of pride. The vow of obedience declares that you are ready to give up your ego, otherwise you can't engage with the joys and woes of others. Every plant, every insect speaks to us, but we do not listen. And yet, religious life is not possible without feeling this connection with all living things.

Why was the Asian Bishops' Conference held here?

In 1990, ten Asian bishops spent eight days here. The meeting caused quite a rumpus, because of the conditions of poverty in our community. Afterwards, the bishops were impressed by the simplicity and contemplation. For example, when a Thai bishop returned to his diocese, he did something quite disruptive. He called the priests and people together and explained that, according to the example he had seen in our community, Mass must be celebrated in contact with the earth. It's not about the intellect, but about the experience! The bishops fasted for three days here, and that, too, caused a fuss, because we in the Church have lost the habit of fasting. Poverty, too, has disappeared. These days, every monastery has what it needs. The joy of poverty is no longer known.

Aren't you idealizing poverty?

(*Fiercely*) No, because we're happy! Our relationship to things is very simple; very mysterious and meaningful, too. Poverty is necessary because when the body is spoilt, or we are enslaved by our intellect or our ego, we cannot lead a spiritual life. For the sake of peace on Earth, some countries must be freed from the arrogance of their ego. Economy needs spirituality, or else everything will fall apart.

THE REMEMBRANCE WOOD

Why have you turned the woods around Takamori Soan into a remembrance wood?

We have erected a cross here for victims who aren't remembered anywhere else. There is also a fountain, fed from three sources, where I baptize people if they want. The fountain represents the water that flowed from Jesus' side when He hung on the cross – even nature enacts this mystery! An embittered Filipino woman whose family had been murdered by the Japanese army came here. She was troubled because, despite her Catholic beliefs, she was unable to forgive. When I walked with her into the wood, she started crying and didn't stop. 'Now, at last, I can forgive,' she said. Her bitterness became liberation. Well, that's the reason for the Church's existence.

BODY

In your letter to me, you called your body your donkey. How do you see the relationship between body and soul?

The body is the base. You may not uncouple your body from your spiritual life, because it is a concrete expression of nature. And yet, you must understand that you must become simple if you want to lead a spiritual life. The body's suffering is also a means of coming into contact with the voice of God. I say this from my own experience, because I have looked death in the eye on a number of occasions and realize that suffering can grant access to the hereafter, however mysterious that might sound. There is no rational explanation. The great mystics often point to the link between suffering and the other world.

ZEN AND CHRISTIANITY

What is the difference between Zen and Christianity?

The difference is historical. Man is the same, his relationship with the numinous is the same. Only the way in which the mystery manifests is different. Jesus is physical and transcendent, while man is arrogant – and so Jesus opted for crucifixion. He wanted to give us a taste of that other world, and as a consequence the Easter mystery, the cross and the resurrection are there for us all!

Turning it around, I could also say that Christ integrated Zen into His life. By that, I mean that Buddhism has no monopoly over Zen, just as Christianity has no monopoly over Christ. I myself grew up in the spirit of Zen, but that, too, is relative, because my true Zen master has been my illness. When I lay at death's door, I realized how selfish my life had been, and that it had to change. That was the beginning of true Zen in my life.

What do you think about Westerners who want to become Buddhists?

I think it's about something else. When I was studying theology and they tried to explain to us about the incarnation of Christ, I felt that everything was based on concepts, ideas about reality. But the rose petal fluttering in the pristine light is more evocative of the real world than any theory. Westerners who practise Zen do not do it from pure curiosity. They are homesick for true reality. Their spiritual need makes them hunger for silence.

What is the difference between Christ and Buddha – or is the distinction merely a conceptual one?

The hereafter is the hereafter. God is God. In the remembrance wood there is a small statue made by a Catholic nurse who came to Japan to learn *zazen*. When she left, she made two statues: one for her Zen master and one for me. It is of the Buddha embracing a small crucified Jesus. 'We have a flock of sheep to care for,' said Jesus, and so there is no difference between Jew and Samaritan, because all is the mercy of God or the Buddha.

When I go to interreligious gatherings, I am always placed on the side of the Buddhists, but I am a Buddhist who has met Christ. Zen monks visit here often, and I am frequently invited to comment on their Buddhist teachings, the sutras. I don't much like to use the word 'dialogue', because it's not about dialogue – it's about meeting at the depths, meeting with reality. Our roots are the same, neither East nor West. Because we are Adam and Eve.

Which problems do you see as most important?

Five rich countries – America, Russia, France, Britain and China – already have nuclear weapons. India and Pakistan are now building them. These countries' leaders proclaim that they are against the use of these weapons, but then why don't they stop building them?

What happened in Hiroshima and Nagasaki, and what is still happening there now, is a drama! At first, the survivors of the atom bomb who went on to have healthy children were relieved, but now it is their grandchildren and their great-grandchildren who are getting leukaemia. It doesn't stop! If nuclear war breaks out, humanity will fall into terrible darkness. The Church has work to do in this: to intervene and get the manufacture of nuclear weapons stopped.

What difference can spirituality make to that?

There is no hope if we don't become humble and simple – because that is the essence of spiritual life. That is why spiritual people are feared: not because they are poor, but because they see so clearly what others, those in power, are doing. As long as the Church is rich, it cannot direct people to take another direction, which is its job. We must serve each other, not dominate each other.

GALILEE

What role do you see for the Church and religion in the twenty-first century?

The law, the teachings of the Church cannot replace true spiritual life. Even meditation in Japan these days has become too institutionalized. We must return to true spirituality, the simplicity of contact with God in our nothingness. Vows express that. We must be prepared to die of hunger on the street as we follow the hand of Jesus. Then we shall see that God gives real, material help. I speak from my own experience. Here in Takamori Soan, although we are poor, we have never had to go without. Throughout my life, I have felt that the hand of God was with us. So the Church should return to Galilee. The risen Christ said, 'I shall meet you in Galilee.'

MAGNIFICENT

Vincent Shigeto died on 6 November 2003 and was buried in Takamori.

His last words were: 'God is magnificent, the Church is magnificent.'
On his headstone is engraved a haiku he wrote himself:

The spring that flows
That flows abundantly,
I bless it, I bless it.

(Last words and haiku taken from Jacques Scheuer, *Enseignements de Vincent Shigeto Oshida*)

18
Timothy Radcliffe

Not afraid of the lions

He can see in the dark. Or so it seems to me, because where Timothy Radcliffe walks with ease, I stumble over obstacles in the cloister of Blackfriars in Oxford at dusk. As we reach the wooden gate that leads from the Dominican garden into the alley, he explains this peculiarity. 'I think it is because as a child I used to play outside in the woods close to our house. I loved the time when dusk would set in because you can watch animals like badgers and foxes leaving their hiding places. So I had to train my eyes to get used to the dark and to be attentive and silent so as not to disturb them.' The qualities Timothy Radcliffe developed are serving him well. Finding his way through the often dimly lit streets of cities all over the world where he is asked to bring his message, requires intuition about how to walk and talk with care.

'Aren't you ever afraid to travel in often dangerous territory?' I ask him. He tells me a recurrent dream he had as a child. He used to wake up at night, terrified because he had once again dreamt that he was going to be attacked by the lions he would surely meet out in the woods. And then, in one dream, he actually met the lions and to his surprise they didn't harm him. 'Once you really meet the difficulties,' he explains, 'they often prove to be far less frightening than you had always thought.'

Defying dangers may well be ingrained in his family. He tells me about his Great Uncle Dick, a Benedictine uncle known as Dom John Lane Fox, who had served as a military chaplain to the British forces during the First World War. At the end of each

201

day in battle in Northern France, he risked his life to bring back the dead and wounded left in no man's land. Perhaps that is what Timothy himself is doing: recovering the wounded of our world from their no man's land of war, hunger and inequality and trying to pull them out of there. Now that the Church itself has committed terrible misdeeds, I wonder what his answers to my questions will be.

UNPRECEDENTED

Is the abuse crisis in the Church unprecedented or has it endured similar shock waves before?

We have never had quite this particular crisis. There have been many crises in the life of the Church and each has been different. The Church passes through periodic crises, but we must not be afraid of them, as every crisis opens the possibility for renewal. We grow up as human beings by going through lots of crises: being born, puberty, adolescence, leaving home, getting married, dying. So being a human being means living through crises. And this is true for the Church as well.

The crises you refer to are normal transitions when growing up; sexual abuse is not part of them.

I agree. It's shocking and terrible. For many of us, certainly for me, the disclosures have come completely unexpectedly. I knew that there had been occasional failures, but I had no idea of the scale. So that was a deep shock. We must be honest and face it and try to live through it.

Is celibacy the problem that has led to sexual abuse?

I don't think so. All the statistics we have for Britain and the United States show that married clergy fail just as often. I think the problem is not celibacy but a form of clericalism where priests in many denominations and in many faiths think that ordination makes them powerful. Abuse is the misuse of power. But in the Gospels, Jesus says that he who leads must serve. I hope this humiliation of the Church will teach us humility and I hope that a new Church will be born which will be much less clerical. We also have to rediscover that the most important sacrament is not ordination but baptism.

RITE OF INITIATION

But a baptized child is not conscious of being baptized.

No, but the child is doing wonderful new things all the time, like learning to walk and talk, without consciously remembering them. Life is a gift to the child, and so is eternal life.

We have to rediscover the profound dignity of baptism. When John Paul II was asked what the most important day of his life was, he answered, 'The day I was baptized.' If we have a really strong sense of the beauty and the dignity of baptism, the Church will flourish.

Do you consider baptism more important than ordination?

Oh yes, absolutely. Baptism is the great sacrament through which you share in Christ's death and resurrection. But its importance is often forgotten because we think that baptism is like getting vaccinated. I have just been to the Sudan and was vaccinated against all sorts of illnesses like rabies and meningitis. But being baptized into the life of God is the most important sacrament you could ever have.

Isn't it arrogant to have a small baby baptized so that it is drawn into the numbers of the Church?

But would it be arrogant for parents to teach their children English rather than leaving them to choose which language to learn? Would it be arrogant for parents to say to a child, 'I will give you no moral training; I will not teach you anything about being good or bad; you have to choose for yourself when you are adult'? That would be crazy! Baptism is about being alive, and any parent wants its child to live. Of course, when the child is old enough it will decide whether it wants to claim its baptism or not.

Can somebody be debaptized?

Not really, no. But you can break with the community.

A lot of people claim the right to debaptism because they are so outraged at the abuse scandal in the Church.

We must understand that anger; it is justified. The first thing is not to defend the Church, but to listen. We have to understand the gravity of what has happened because childhood is fundamental to being a human being. Monkeys have very short childhoods, chickens have almost no childhood at all. Human beings, by contrast, have a long childhood so that they can grow and acquire character. Childlikeness remains a permanent characteristic of any mature adult human being. That's why the abuse of children is so terrible – because it not only damages a young person, it attacks the root of their humanity.

Do you see any possibilities for baptism to be restored?

I think so. In the 1970s, a new rite for the Christian initiation of adults was introduced which is very widely used now. The word 'initiation', meaning 'beginning', is beautiful. God is always fresh, always young, always new. Baptism is initiating people into God's eternal newness. We may have a big crisis, but, in Britain at least, we have many converts to Catholicism.

Many come from atheism, some from other forms of Christianity. There are quite a few Muslims converting to Christianity, but we don't talk about that because often it would endanger their lives.

We are more aware that baptism is not just a private thing for parents and their children. Through baptism you are brought into the community of the Church. I am very lucky to be one of six siblings, but I really have millions, billions of brothers and sisters by baptism.

THE MEDIA

It is said that the abuse crisis is being used by the media to discredit the Church as a whole. Do you agree?

We must resist the temptation to blame the media. In some ways they have forced us to face our failure and we must be grateful for that. It's true that some people will use this crisis to attack the Church. But we need to be conscious that it's not the media's fault, but ours.

Nonetheless, the media have been biased in some cases. Does their role need to be reassessed?

There is indeed a real problem about the power of the media. The media are often untruthful. That is a tragedy because it undermines the bonds of human society. Politicians fear that if they confront the media, they will be destroyed. The accountability of the media is a real problem, not only for the Church but for the whole of society.

A PARODY

The Church, in advocating forgiveness, can provide an easy way out for abusers. Perpetrators can suit themselves, knowing they will be forgiven!

That is a complete parody of forgiveness. That would be to turn forgiveness into irresponsibility. It would destroy us as moral agents who have to accept responsibility for what we have done and what we have been. Forgiveness is not forgetting your wrongdoings. That would be to trivialize them. On the contrary, it means daring to remember what you have done and not despair. Forgiveness is accepting to be transformed and changed by God's love.

Can everything be forgiven?

If you are open to receive it.

Doesn't the victim have to agree to forgiveness as well?

Often, asking for the forgiveness of those whom we have harmed is an important part of asking for God's forgiveness. If I steal from you, it does not make much sense to ask for God's forgiveness unless I give you back your money! But it is not always possible to receive the forgiveness of others. They may be dead or refuse it.

Can God forgive everything?

God simply loves us. He doesn't have a list of things He can forgive – His love is healing. It's not sweeping something under the carpet either. We have to stand by the victims; we cannot demand their forgiveness. We cannot expect anything until we have listened and given them time to express themselves.

Doesn't the perpetrator have to pass through a period of remorse?

Absolutely. Remorse is intrinsic. If you have no remorse, you are not accepting God's forgiveness.

THE FORCE

Isn't Christianity an old and dying religion?

It depends on where you are. At the beginning of the twentieth century, two thirds of all Christians were from Europe and North America, whereas today, two thirds of Christians are from Asia, Latin America and Africa. In these continents, Christianity is flourishing and is an enormous force for challenging unjust structures.

In the south of Sudan, Christianity is the main functioning structure! In the south-west, which I visited, the Catholic Church provides education, health care, food distribution, training in citizens' rights, radio broadcasts. Globally, the Church is by far the biggest organization for health care and education. About a third of all health care in the world is provided by the Church.

The idea that Christianity is a spent force, disappearing down the plughole, is simply untrue. This is a time of enormous vitality for Christianity. And we live in a global Catholic Church. I recently went to Vancouver, where I met priests from India, Sri Lanka, Vietnam, Nigeria and Holland. So in a global world, the Church is by far the most globalized institution there is. Even in China there appear to be more Christians than Communists! In the whole of Asia, there are now more Christians than Buddhists.

And in Europe? You are in contact with many students in Oxford. What evolution do you see?

I think it's true that we are moving to a smaller Church in Europe, but it would be a great mistake to think that there is no new life. If you go to church here in Oxford you will find many students attending Sunday Mass. Many youngsters are turning to Christianity to explore questions about their lives.

I've just finished rereading the wonderful *Anna Karenina* by Tolstoy. The main character, Levin, who is always struggling with existential questions such as what it means to be a human being, meets an old peasant who tells him that you don't live for yourself. And suddenly Levin experiences a wonderful moment of illumination. Right at the end of the book, he begins to understand his faith for the first time. I recognize many young people in Tolstoy's protagonist. They are asking questions like: 'Who am I? What does it mean to be a human being? What is human happiness? What are we made for?' And if we can engage with those people and their questions, the Church will have a future in Europe too.

What is most striking in the countries you have visited lately? Do you favour some continents more than others?

I usually go to the United States two or three times a year. This year, I have been to Sudan, Ethiopia, Sri Lanka, Indonesia, Singapore and some countries in Latin America as well. The old domination of the West is coming to an end and we see a new world being born. China, Indonesia, India, Brazil are the growing economies, whereas Europe and America are losing their dominance. This is so within the Church as well.

I love going to Asia because there is so much vitality. When I was in Indonesia, I was asked to meet some young Catholic professionals in Jakarta. I imagined there would be about 30 of them, but there were 600, and they were all Chinese! I also gave a retreat for the bishops and the priests, all arranged by lay people. At the beginning of the retreat, the woman who organized it addressed them, saying, 'I want you to be holier. You are not holy enough! And that is why we arranged this retreat for you. I will check up in six months to see if you are really better!' The Church in Asia is in many ways more relaxed than in Europe!

WE ARE NOT FINISHED

Dominicans can hold very different, sometimes opposing, opinions, but what should they agree on? What keeps you together?

We would all agree that the truth is to be sought in debate and discussion. Disagreeing with somebody is not a problem but an opportunity. If we pray and study the scriptures, and are intelligent and charitable in our debates, we can move together towards truth. What is really distinctive in the Dominican life is that we have Chapters where we reflect on what we want to do and how we must live together. This form of democracy has remained unchanged for almost 800 years. We follow the rule of St Augustine, which has only very few prescriptions because it is more of a spiritual document. And then there are the constitutions of the Order, which we can change. So built into the very identity of the Order is the capacity to change!

Do Dominicans still have any appeal in this day and age?

I think so. Every year we have hundreds of young men and women who join us. We have had our ups and downs, but in the New York Province, one of just four in the United States, we have 21 novices for this year, and many in Ireland. We are not finished. We have many vocations in Nigeria, the Philippines and Vietnam, and in Europe we're not finished either. We recently had a day for vocations here in Blackfriars, and 12 young men were interested. They probably won't all join, but some will.

In some places, like Spain and Italy, we presently have few vocations, but the only places that I know of where there has been none for years are Holland and the Flemish part of Belgium. I think there has been a loss of confidence in religious life in these countries. There is a revival however in the French-speaking part of Belgium. In Louvain-la-Neuve and Liège we have even opened new communities this year, and adjacent to the priories we have opened Blackfriars bars. With a lot of success!

IN A PUB

Aren't Dominicans presumptuous? In order to preach you must be convinced you possess the truth!

(*Laughing*) It is no coincidence that St Dominic founded the Order in a pub, because there is no preaching without listening!

When I became a university chaplain, I was convinced that I would be a wonderful preacher. But I discovered that the students were bored stiff during my sermons. Here I was, a young preacher who didn't know how to preach! So, I invited the students to go to a pub with me after evening Mass on Sunday and asked them to tell me what was wrong with my preaching, and they did! I discovered that I had to listen before I spoke. Some of us met beforehand, talked about the Gospel and prepared the sermon together. It was an important experience for me because it meant that I, as a preacher, had to listen first. If you preach at people, and think you've got the truth all wrapped up, then you are indeed arrogant and ineffective as well.

What makes somebody a good preacher?

You have to find your own voice. Each of us is a word of God, but a different word of God! The word of God has passed through your own individual humanity, which means you must speak as the person you are, and say only what you believe to be true, not because you're expected to say it.

And if that's opposite to what the Catholic Church believes to be true...?

We teach the Catholic faith, but the Catholic faith is very broad. Orthodoxy is a big, open space. You cannot use the pulpit to campaign for your own personal views on controversial topics.

Nevertheless, opinions may diverge substantially on celibacy, women priests, civil partnerships!

All these questions are very important, but the sermon is not the place to take a line. You need debate, articles in newspapers and discussions, whereas the sermon is the moment to share your faith. It would be a betrayal to use the pulpit as a party-political broadcast.

One of the problems of the Church is the deep splits and divisions between conservative and progressive, traditionalist and liberal. These categories originated during the eighteenth century Enlightenment, which asserted that progress was always a liberation from tradition, and especially from Catholic dogma. But for Catholics, this opposition of tradition and progress is unhelpful. The tradition – the Gospels and the teaching of the Church – renew us and propel us forward to new insights. And so we must refuse these labels. The prophetic task at the moment is to overcome that division.

BETRAYING THE BREADTH OF CATHOLICISM

Even so, we operate according to these labels! It seems to be engrained in our society.

I know, and it drives me crazy because I am always reading that I am a progressive.

Aren't you a progressive?

I admit that I am, but I am also a traditionalist, because the two are not incompatible. In all honesty, I am a bit of both. I love tradition, I love history, I love the wealth that we receive from the past, but I also love the future. Some people are temperamentally more inclined to cherish the past, like my mother, while others are more fascinated with the new, like my father, but that's not a fundamental opposition; it's not a dichotomy; it's a question of temperament.

Now, some people become ideologically conservative or ideologically progressive, which is quite different. When it becomes ideological, you'll say, 'I have truth wrapped up.' But no one can own the truth. That is an arrogance. God is always beyond our concepts.

We are necessarily traditionalist. We receive the Gospels, the teaching of the Church, figures like St Paul, Augustine, Thomas

Aquinas, from the past. But you could not be a Catholic without being progressive as well, because you have to long for the Kingdom, for justice, for the abolition of suffering. Somebody who's ideologically traditionalist or ideologically progressive would be betraying the breadth of Catholicism.

Many people in the Church are grieving a loss. Until you understand their pain, you won't be able to talk to them. Many traditionalists mourn the death of the old Church they loved. Sometimes I am not entirely sure that Church really existed, but there is a lot of nostalgia among young Catholics for a Church they never knew. The book *Brideshead Revisited* by Evelyn Waugh, set in romantic Oxford, is a good example of such nostalgia. But the liberals are grieving too. They are mourning the loss of the progressive Church that they thought was coming after Vatican II and they now see a Church which is becoming more clerical. If we understand each other's sorrows and joys, we can begin to talk.

So, we have to resist using these categories, we have to be countercultural. The split in the Church between traditionalists and progressives is a sign that we are not being countercultural, but that we have accepted the values of society instead.

In challenging this mentality, some of the first things we need are imagination and understanding. 'Why does this person treasure the Tridentine rite? Why does somebody else want to have a Mass with a guitar in?' Only if I imaginatively grasp what they love, will I be able to understand them.

So do we have to find another word to express this in-between position?

Well, it's not an in-between position. You see, the Vatican Council was a wonderful step forward, it was also a step back to the Gospel. It's not in between. You go forward and you go back. The important question is not, 'Is it progressive or is it conservative?' The important question is, 'Is it true?'

How do you know?

Because you study, you think, you pray and you talk. You study the Gospels, you study the tradition, you pray for illumination, you argue with people and hope you will learn.

What happens if opinions on truth diverge?

Well, what do you see in the Gospels? Jesus was always a man of conversation. St John's Gospel is a sequence of conversations with Nicodemus, the woman at the well, the blind man, the disciples at the end, Pontius Pilate. You constantly see Jesus engaging in conversation. Fundamental to the mission of the Church, to the pursuit of truth, is that we converse. Some people get nervous at that idea because they say, 'Dialogue is relativistic. Where is the proclamation? Where is the conversion?' But the word in English for a sermon is 'homily', which is Greek for 'conversation'. A homily is literally a conversation; it springs out of the dialogue of the community and is at the service of that conversation which holds the community together.

It doesn't look like that to me.

No, it doesn't always look like that, but it is to be part of the conversation of the whole church. And if you have a good conversation, you both change. I often think about my brother Pierre Claverie. He engaged all his life in conversation with Islam and it changed him. He became a better, deeper Christian. And the conversation changed his audience. Some of them became better Muslims and some better Christians.

STUDY OR ACTION?

What is most important for Dominicans: study or social action?

A lot of the Dominicans, like Godfrey Nzamujo or Henri Burin des Roziers are engaged in social action, but there are thousands of Dominicans whose fundamental life is that of study, which is extraordinarily exciting, as Katarina Pajchel, a young nun who is part of a research group working for CERN, demonstrates. St Thomas Aquinas, in a story that is probably apocryphal, said to a young friar, 'You must remain in your room and study if you want to enter the wine cellar!' What could be more attractive for a young Dominican than getting into the wine cellar? The joy of understanding! Many of the brothers who are engaged in social action know this. I once asked Pedro Meca, a Spanish Dominican living with tramps on the streets of Paris, how he survives, and he answered, 'Because I studied St Thomas Aquinas!' Good study brings you down to earth!

What could a street worker like Pedro learn from Thomas Aquinas?

He didn't tell me, but I would guess it is Aquinas' deep optimism. Thomas Aquinas has a very hopeful view of being human, and a wonderful understanding of human freedom. He sees the whole of human life as a journey to happiness. So, he gave Pedro the foundation to live happily even on the streets.

Another example of a close relationship between study and action is when the first friars arrived in La Española (today Haiti and the Dominican Republic). Bartolomé de Las Casas, Antonio de Montesinos and Pedro de Cordoba were the first people to stand up for the humanity of the Indians and to respect their culture. But they were always in dialogue with their brothers at the University of Salamanca in Spain, like Domingo de Soto and Francisco de Vitoria. De Vitoria was the first person to evolve an understanding of international human rights. His statue can be seen in Geneva at the Human Rights Commission! He was an academic and Las Casas was on the ground, but they were always communicating because Las Casas needed the intellectual vitality of De Vitoria, who in turn needed the living experience of Las Casas. They were inseparable.

LIVING AMONG MUSLIMS

In a disturbing interview I had with the Iraqi sister Maria Hanna she said about Islam, 'Europe doesn't know what's coming.' Sister Faustina from Nigeria voiced the same fears. Is the old hostility between Muslims and Christians back?

Nobody knows what is coming. We don't know how far Islam will be able to adapt and change in the European context. We don't know how it will be possible to be a young, convinced Muslim in a liberal democratic society.

Personally, I am optimistic because I meet many bright young Muslims at Oxford and Cambridge Universities and many of them are wonderful and have much to give.

When Christianity encountered modernity and had to accept historical criticism of the Bible, it was painful, but modernity was at least the fruit of Christianity. It is more difficult for Islam. For us Christians, the word of God is the encounter with a person. We have texts but, certainly in the Catholic tradition, we are not fundamentalist about the texts because the word of God is, above all, a person.

In Islam, the Koran is believed to be the unchangeable revealed word of God, so it makes it much more difficult to understand how to criticize the text historically. There have been times in the history of Islam when this aspect was debated. We have to be very close to our Islamic brothers and sisters and try to help them face the challenges of modernity. And we have to understand their criticisms of the West, which are sometimes justified, like their critique of loose sexual morality, for instance. I think Pope Benedict has been good on this. We have both to encourage Muslims to belong to our modern Western society and understand and engage with their criticisms of our society, which are sometimes valid.

CONTEMPLATIVES

During the time I spent in Dominican contemplative monasteries, I wondered what sense it makes to lock yourself up? Isn't it 'other worldly'?

We are all very tempted to run away from ourselves and create false images of who we are. Our celebrity culture creates false images of people and then destroys them. People living the monastic life have to live with themselves inescapably. They have to be face to face with themselves in the presence of God. That's not other worldly, it is very 'this worldly'. Nuns are facing the truth of themselves in the presence of God. Many people like to visit monasteries because they are places of truthfulness about the human condition.

Isn't it a selfish way of living? Isn't it better to give soup to the poor than to pray as the medieval Dominican Meister Eckhart suggested?

Meister Eckhart was a great mystic and spent hours in prayer, but if somebody appeared at the door he would answer the visitor's needs.

I think the role of the contemplative nuns in the preaching of the Order is very important. In the early days of the Order, the preachers stayed with them. When St Dominic went to Rome, he lived with the nuns until the brethren started making too much noise coming back late at night. Then the nuns were relieved, I am sure, when the brethren found their own place to live!

But the link with the nuns has always been there. The friars go there when they want to rest, to pray and to be renewed. Besides, the very life of the nuns is a preaching. We are always tempted to think that we are valuable because of what we achieve. These nuns preach to us because they show human life is valuable in itself. They witness the absolute priority of God. What better witness to the beauty of the monastic life than the film *Des hommes et des Dieux* (directed by Xavier Beauvois, 2010)?

RENEWAL

What is the relationship of the Order with the lay Dominicans? Aren't you afraid they will try to push the Order in the direction they want to take?

I hope so! I hope that the nuns, the sisters and the brothers will all try to push us in the direction they think important; but we have to do this together. Unity in the Order is very important for us. We preach the Kingdom of God in which humanity will be united, and so it would make no sense to have an Order of Preachers that was divided.

At present, there are probably about 200,000 lay Dominicans and they have very different styles of life, as you can see from the lay Dominicans in prison in Norfolk, who bring hope to their fellow intimates, the Vietnamese lay Dominicans who preach where the brethren cannot go, academic lay Dominicans, or musicians like James MacMillan. I think the main challenge for the brethren is to give them the time they need for formation. We are always tempted to think that we are too busy.

I think the crucial question of the Church today is lay leadership, rooted in baptism. So we need lay Dominicans who will be lay leaders, and that requires a good theological formation to understand their specific role. It's bad enough to have the clericalization of the Church, it would be even worse to have the clericalization of the laity!

We must bear in mind that renewal of the Church has often come through the laity. Who are the three great patron saints of Europe? St Benedict, St Francis of Assisi and St Catherine of Siena. And what do they have in common? None of them were ordained. So, we must have confidence in the vitality of lay people. When Blessed John Henry Newman was asked what he thought of the laity, he replied that the Church would look rather foolish without them!

Bibliography and further reading

Timothy Radcliffe

By him:
- *I Call You Friends*, Continuum, London, 2003.
- *Seven Last Words*, Continuum, London, 2004.
- *Sing a New Song: The Christian Vocation*, Dominican Publications, Dublin, 1999.
- *What is the Point of Being a Christian?*, Continuum, London, 2005.
- *Why Go to Church? The Drama of the Eucharist*, Continuum, London, 2008 (The Archbishop of Canterbury's Lent Book 2009).

Aniceto Fernández, Vincent de Couesnongle, Damian Byrne, Timothy Radcliffe, *To Praise, to Bless, to Preach: Words of Grace and Truth*, Dominican Publications, Dublin, 2004.

Timothy Radcliffe (ed.), *Just One Year: Prayer and Worship through the Christian Year*, Darton, Longman and Todd for CAFOD and Christian Aid, London, 2006.

Timothy Radcliffe with Lytta Basset and Eric Fassin, *Christians and Sexuality in the Time of AIDS*, Continuum, London, 2008.

Also mentioned:
- D. H. Lawrence, *A Propos of Lady Chatterley's Lover*, London, 1931 (pamphlet).
- Barack Obama, *Dreams from My Father: A Story of Race and Inheritance*, Three Rivers Press, New York, 2004.

- Simon Tugwell, *Early Dominicans: Selected Writings*, Paulist Press, New Jersey, 1982.

Jean-Jacques Pérennès

Jean-Jacques Pérennès, *A Life Poured Out: Pierre Claverie of Algeria*, Orbis Books, Maryknoll, New York, 2007.

Jean-Jacques Pérennès, Georges Anawati (1905–1994): *Un chrétien égyptien devant le mystère de l'Islam*, Les Editions du Cerf, Paris, 2008.

James MacMillan

Selected Musical works

Búsqueda, music theatre work, setting texts from the Latin Mass and poems by the Argentinean Mothers of the Disappeared, 1988.

Cantos Sagrados, for choir and orchestra, 1989/1997.

Fourteen Little Pictures, for piano trio, 1997.

Parthenogenesis, scena, in collaboration with Dr Rowan Williams, libretto by Michael Symmons Roberts, 2000.

Seven Last Words from the Cross, cantata for choir and strings, 1993.

St John Passion, for baritone, choir and orchestra, 2007.

'*Tremunt Videntes Angelis*', setting of fifth-century Latin hymn 'Aeterne rex altissime', for unaccompanied choir, 2001.

Triduum, triptych for orchestra, 1997: The World's Ransoming, concerto for cor Anglais and orchestra; Concerto for Cello and Orchestra, commissioned by Rostropovich; Symphony: Vigil, commissioned by Rostropovich.

Veni, Veni, Emmanuel, percussion concerto, 1992.

Visitatio Sepulchri, music theatre work, setting texts from fourteenth-century Easter Day liturgical drama, 1993.

Commissioned for the UK visit of Pope Benedict XVI in September 2010:
* *Mass of Blessed John Henry Newman*
* 'Tu es Petrus', introit for the Papal Mass at Westminster Cathedral
* 'Gospel Fanfare', for choir, organ, brass and percussion.

Brian Pierce

Brian J. Pierce, *Martin de Porres: A Saint of the Americas*, Liguori Publications, Liguori, Missouri, 2004.

Brian J. Pierce, *We Walk the Path Together: Learning from Thich Nhat Hanh and Meister Eckhart*, Orbis Books, Maryknoll, New York, 2005.

Maria Hanna

Maria Hanna, *Drawn by Love: A history of the Dominican Sisters of St Catherine of Siena, Mosul, Iraq*, Sor Juana Press, (English and Arabic), San Antonio, Texas, 2010.

Henri Burin des Roziers

Bernardete Toneto *Frère Henri Burin des Roziers, avocat des sans-terre*, Les Editions du Cerf, Paris, 2002.

Godfrey Nzamujo

Godfrey Nzamujo, *Songhaï: Quand l'Afrique relève la tête*, Les Editions du Cerf, Paris, 2002.

Helen Alford

Helen J. Alford, Charles Clark, S. A. Cortright, Michael J. Naughton (eds), *Rediscovering Abundance: Interdisciplinary Essays on Wealth, Income and their Distribution in the Catholic Social Tradition*, University of Notre Dame Press, Notre Dame, Indiana, 2006.

Helen J. Alford and Michael J. Naughton, *Managing as if Faith Mattered: Christian Social Principles in the Modern Organization*, University of Notre Dame Press, Notre Dame, Indiana, 2001.

Charles M. A. Clark and Sr Helen Alford, *Rich and Poor: Rebalancing the Economy*, Catholic Truth Society, London, 2010.

Francesco Compagnoni and Helen Alford (eds), *Preaching Justice: Dominican Contributions to Social Ethics in the Twentieth Century*, Dominican Publications, Dublin, 2007.

Suzanne Noffke, *Catherine of Siena: The Dialogue*, Paulist Press, New York, 1980.

Katarina Pajchel

Simon Tugwell, *The Way of the Preacher*, Darton, Longman and Todd, London, 1979.

Simone Weil, *Waiting for God*, Harper Perennial, London, 2001.

Emilio Platti

Abdelwahab Meddeb, *La maladie de l'Islam*, Editions du Seuil, Paris, 2002.

Emilio Platti, *Christian-Muslim Relations: A bibliographical history, Volume 2*, Brill, Leiden, Boston 2009.

Emilio Platti, *Islam, Friend or Foe?*, Louvain Theological and Pastoral Monographs, Peeters, Leuven, 2008.

Kim En Joong

Books of his paintings:
- *Bruxelles-Paris: Exhibitions expositions du jubilé de l'an 2000*, Les Editions du Cerf, Paris, 2000.
- *Kim En Joong,* Les Editions du Cerf, Paris, 1997.
- *Les Retrouvailles*, Les Editions du Cerf, Paris, 2002.

- *Paris-Tokyo-Séoul 2004,* Editions du Cerf-Yeobaek, Paris-Seoul, 2004.
- *Résonnances,* Les Editions du Cerf, Paris, 2007.
- *Vitraux – Stained Glass,* Les Editions du Cerf, Paris, 2009.

Christiane Keller and Joël Damase, *Brioude: La basilique de Saint-Julien dans la lumière de Kim En Joong,* Les Editions du Cerf, Paris, 2009.

Jean Thuillier, *Kim En Joong: Peintre de Lumière,* Les Editions du Cerf, Paris, 2004.

Jean-Noël Christiani, *Face au Ciel, un documentaire avec Kim En Joong,* Yumi Productions, Paris, 2009.

Breda Carroll

Walter J. Ciszek, *He Leadeth Me,* Ignatius Press, San Francisco, 1995.

Suzanne Noffke, *Catherine of Siena: The Dialogue,* Paulist Press, New York, 1980.

Vincent Shigeto Oshida

Katrin Amell, *Contemplation et Dialogue: Quelques examples de dialogue entre spiritualités après le concile Vatican II,* The Swedish Institute of Missionary Research, Uppsala, 1998.

Jacques Scheuer, *Enseignements de Vincent Shigeto Oshida (1922–2003), un Maître Zen qui a rencontré le Christ,* Voies de l'Orient, Brussels, 2009.